CARTER'S COAST OF NEW ENGLAND

WHITE HEAD, NEAR PORTLAND

CARTER'S
Coast of
New England

A New Edition of
A Summer Cruise on the Coast of New England
by Robert Carter

Edited and with a foreword
by Daniel Ford

New Hampshire Publishing Company
Somersworth
1977

Library of Congress Catalog Card Number 75-18528

International Standard Book Number 0-912274-53-0

New Hampshire Publishing Company, Somersworth 03878

© 1969, 1977 by the New Hampshire Publishing Company

Printed in the United States of America

FOREWORD

Some voyages are eternal. When Richard Henry Dana shipped out before the mast, when Charles Darwin joined the *Beagle* expedition, when Joshua Slocum single-handed the *Spray* around the world—they sailed not once, but as many times as there are readers who love the sea.

To this fine company I would add the name of Robert Carter, who sailed aboard the sloop *Helen* in the summer of 1858, from Boston to Provincetown, along the brief New Hampshire shore, and down the coast of Maine.

Carter was a journalist, and he wrote about the trip for his employer, the *New York Tribune*. In 1864 his dispatches were collected under the title *A Summer Cruise on the Coast of New England*, published by Crosby and Nichols in Boston. In 1889 a British edition was published by Alexander Gardner in London.

The book was allowed to languish after that—unpublished but not unsold. It would not be too much to say that it went underground. From libraries and secondhand stores and attic collections, it returned to circulation as sailors discovered that—next to the *Coast Pilot* itself—the most essential reading in New England waters was the story of a cruise made more than a century before. By the time I happened upon him, Robert Carter was fetching up to twenty-five dollars in the antiquarian bookstores. It was a fate such as every author dreams of, especially those (the vast majority) who do not achieve bestsellerdom in their own lifetimes.

Still, the coast of New England is but a fragment of the world's geography, and sailors are but a fragment of the bookseller's market. Thus it was that "Carter's Coast" remained a collector's item until 1969, when three of us decided to revive it for the bright new world that has replaced the one Robert Carter knew, and which values lobsters at several dollars apiece instead of the three cents that Carter paid.

As editor, I slimmed the text by removing some of its nineteenth-century luggage of semi-colons and literary quotations. An artist found the wood engravings to illustrate Carter's voyage. And a printer assembled it in time for the Boston Globe Book Festival in October, bearing the colophon of the New Hampshire Publishing Company. It was a heady experience. Either because they were sailors themselves, or because they liked the look of it, the festival managers put *Carter's Coast of New England* right up there with the autumn bestsellers, ten feet tall on a revolving display.

I don't remember what other titles were thus honored. Probably you wouldn't remember them either. But Robert Carter has continued to prosper, going through two printings before returning underground. At the New Hampshire Publishing Company (which has likewise prospered) the orders still come in, three years after the last copy was sold.

Thus this new edition of a book that refuses to die— in paper covers this time, to subdue the ravages of inflation.

This was Robert Carter's only book. He was born in Albany, N.Y., in 1819, and his first literary effort was a poem which was published in an Albany newspaper. It was so badly misprinted that he took to writing prose instead. He spent most of his life in journalism, as Washington correspondent for the *New York Tribune,* and as editor of the *Rochester Democrat, Appleton's Journal,* and the *American Cyclopedia.* Between times he helped establish two cultural phenomena. One was a literary magazine which survived only a short time. The other was the Republican party, which was still going strong when Robert Carter died in 1879.

As for his shipmates on that immortal cruise, they have been identified by F.M. O'Brien, antiquarian bookseller of Portland and one of Carter's many admirers. O'Brien happened upon a first edition, inscribed by "the Professor" in 1865 and naming all who were aboard:

The Professor was Dr. William Stimpson, who joined the North Pacific expedition at the age of twenty, and who spent many years thereafter classifying the materials he gathered. His works were published by the Smithsonian Institution.

The Artist was a certain Henry Carey, who is otherwise unidentified.

And the thirsty Assyrian was Francis Henry Underwood. Lawyer, editor, novelist, and consular official, he helped establish the *Atlantic Monthly* as the voice of the anti-slavery movement in New England.

DANIEL FORD

CONTENTS

1

THE PLAN OF THE CRUISE

On one of the hottest evenings of the hot month of June, 1858, I paid a visit to my friend Professor ————, at his residence on G Street, Washington.

I do not know that my friend had any regular or official claim to the title of Professor. It was conferred upon him by the officers of the North Pacific Exploring Expedition, of which he was Naturalist. They dubbed him Professor of Marine Zoology, in recognition of his skill in the knowledge of all that pertains to the creatures that inhabit the great deep. The study of the ocean and its inhabitants had been a passion with him from early boyhood, and was pursued with such success, that, in 1849, while yet a youth, he had discovered the principle of the aquarium, and had a number of aquariums in successful operation long before anything was heard of the kindred experiments of the Englishman Warrington.

It was a fearfully hot night; one of a long succession of hot nights and days through which I had patiently sweltered and sweated, in the vain expectation that time would gradually accustom me to being broiled and parboiled, as they are said to render eels tolerant of being skinned alive. But a frame acclimated to the moderate heats and invariably cool nights of the seacoast of Massachusetts, could not readily become insensible to an atmosphere which at midnight, as well as at noonday, maintained a heat greater than the average heat of the torrid zone. I sought refuge at the Professor's, because his house, though not materially cooler than the rest of the city, was intellectually and imaginatively cooler. It abounded in objects suggestive of refreshing ideas. There were crabs and shells that had been dragged from the sunless depths of the Arctic Ocean; fishing-lines and dredges that had explored the cool abysses of Kamtchatkan and Siberian seas; drawings of icebergs and glaciers; and, what particularly was wont to give an agreeable chill to my fancy, a picture of the prodigious snowy cone of the great Japanese volcano, Fujiyama, made by a native artist at Simoda, where the Professor himself purchased it.

The Professor, with nothing on but a shirt and the thinnest of trousers, was stretched on a sofa with a cigar in his mouth, languidly smoking, and contemplating through his gold spectacles the ungainly proportions of a monstrous bug he had just captured. Our conversation opened, of course, on the weather.

"I cannot stand it any longer," he said; "I shall start on a cruise on the coast of Maine next week, and you had better come along, if you do not want to die of a fever. You look horribly bilious already, and a few days more of this heat will use you up entirely. Let us go and cool off at Grand Manan.

I spent two months there some summers ago, fishing and dredging, and can assure you that it is the finest place on our whole coast."

"For crabs, I suppose, Professor. All places are classified by you for good or bad with relation to their production of crabs."

"For crabs, yes, but not alone for crabs. The scenery is superb. Huge, rocky cliffs, a thousand feet high, rise right out of deep water, and are broken into the wildest and most romantic caves and inlets. They are the haunt of nearly all kinds of sea-birds, from the herring-gull down to Mother Carey's chickens. We shall catch there and on our way down the coast every species of fish that swims in our seas."

"Including the whale?"

"The whale is not a fish," responded the Professor, gravely, "but I promise you we shall see whales in abundance. We shall also catch sharks, and kill seals and porpoises. But, in short, if you will come along, we will run into every harbor from Provincetown to Eastport, and fish and dredge till you have seen at least one specimen of every creature that swims the sea or dwells on the bottom."

"But how shall we go to the Grand Manan?" I asked.

The Professor's hint about my bilious appearance had privately decided me to take an abrupt leave of the national capital. I already felt a fever in my veins.

"I have written to my friend Tufts, the aqua-

15

rium maker and stocker at Swampscott, to engage me a good, clean, stout fishing-smack of from ten to twenty tons, and also two experienced boat-men, one of them, if possible, old Captain Widger, who went with me on my cruise last year. I shall hear from Tufts in a day or two, and you had better get ready at once, for I shall be off like a flash the moment I can get away."

In reply to my inquiries into the nature and extent of the requisite preparations for a cruise of a month's duration, the Professor said:

"Put two pairs of trousers, two thick coats, and a vest or two, the oldest and worse you have, into a bag — a gunny-bag or a potato-sack will do. Put in, also, a couple of flannel shirts and drawers, and half a dozen or a dozen of thick woollen socks, and an old felt hat. Buy a couple of the thickest red-flannel shirts you can find, a pair of thick-soled cowhide boots, a tight-fitting cloth cap, a cheap straw hat, and a pair of oilskin or India-rubber trousers — oilskin is best, for it doesn't smell so abominably as India-rubber. Put these, with two or three pairs of old slippers, in the bag, and tie it up tight. Put a couple of linen shirts and a de-cent suit of light summer clothes, in a valise, so that you can go ashore at Salem, Portland, East-port, and other civilized places, and see your friends if you have any. That is all the outfit you will need. I will look out for supplying the vessel with pro-visions and table-ware."

"And the damage?"

The Professor has an abhorrence of slang phrases, except those which he uses himself.

"I suppose you mean the expense," he replied. "I cannot exactly tell till I hear from Tufts what sort of craft he has engaged, and on what terms; but if we get one or two others to go and share expenses, the 'damage,' as you call it, will be from $50 to $100 apiece."

This was satisfactory, and I made my preparations accordingly. I put nothing in the bag beyond what the Professor indicated, except a pair of India-rubber overshoes, which I subsequently found of essential service when the deck was too wet for slippers, as was frequently the case.

Two or three days later the Professor came to see me in high glee, intense delight gleaming through the perspiration that rolled down his face from the heat of a walk in the sunshine. He flourished an open letter in his hand.

"Tufts writes that he has engaged the sloop Helen and her owner, Captain Gurney, and that Captain Widger will go if we want him. The sloop was built for a yacht, is stout and tight and roomy, with four berths. She measures thirty-three feet and draws five and half feet of water; has not been much used for fishing, and is consequently clean and in good condition."

"The price?" I suggested.

"Seven dollars and a half a day, including the two men. I shall write to have her brought to Boston on Friday next, and we will start the next day."

BOSTON
AND
ADJACENT CITIES.

2

I was in Boston on the day indicated, Saturday, July 3, and found the sloop, which was moored on the north side of Long Wharf.

The Professor was on board, in a state of keen impatience, accompanied by his friend Tufts, the aquarium stocker of Swampscott, to which port we had decided first to direct our course, to make certain necessary arrangements. The lines were cast off as soon as I touched her deck, and in a few minutes she was going with wind and tide down Boston Harbor, accompanied by a crowd of other craft, of all classes and dimensions, including two or three steamers bound for Baltimore and Philadelphia.

We had gone but five or six miles when the breeze died away and we threw over a cod-line, baited with a clam, in hope of catching something for supper. But we pulled up only a seaweed, consisting of a long, cylindrical, hollow stem, gradually expanding into a leaf some ten inches in breadth. This plant is called by our fishermen and sailors the "Devil's-Apron." Clinging to roots of this weed was a horse-muscle, as large as a man's hand, which, together with small pebbles, had served as an anchor to keep it at the bottom.

The Professor grasped with avidity the roots of the weed. After looking at it attentively a few minutes, he pointed out to me about a dozen snake-armed starfish wound around the tendrils of the roots.

"This species," he said, "is found only in deep water, and can only be got by dredging. It consists, you will observe, of a small central disk of about the size of a ten-cent piece, and five long, slender, spiny arms, which twine like serpents among the roots of the sea-weed. They are often very brilliant, and beautifully variegated in color. Most commonly the disk is red, with a pentagonal white spot in the middle, while the arms are ringed with red and brown."

The Professor next pointed out upon the dripping mass something that looked like a large drop of blood. This, he said, was an ascidian. These ascidians depend for food on what the water floats into their mouths. They pass their old age in a quiet, sedentary way, attached to sea-plants, from which they never separate except by force. In youth, on the contrary, while in the tadpole state, they are continually swimming about till they find a place in which to fix their permanent abode, when the tail of the tadpole disappears and the creature assumes its proper form and leads its proper life.

We found about twenty species of marine animals, and several marine plants besides, on this one piece of seaweed, accidentally pulled from the bottom.

The wind was so light that at 8 p.m. we were only ten miles from Boston, off Nahant. A thick fog coming in from the ocean shut out everything from view. We stood on, however, through a heavy rolling sea, which our Pilot, as we called Captain Widger, said was caused by the fog, though he could

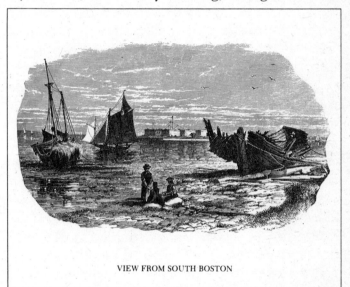

VIEW FROM SOUTH BOSTON

not tell why. The Nahant steamboat, the Nelly Baker, was also caught in the fog, and was blowing a horn at intervals of three or four minutes, and was answered by a horn on shore to direct her to the landing-place. Presently we heard the breakers on Nahant Point, and hauling up to the northward, we soon saw the red light on Egg Rock feebly glimmering through the gloom before us at no great distance. We slowly passed close to the rock, of whose light we lost sight when we were about an eighth of a mile from it, so dense was the fog; and soon after 9 p.m., the wind ceasing entirely, we came to anchor in the bay of Swampscott, about a mile from the shore, in six fathoms of water.

We could see nothing and hear nothing but the roar of the breakers on Egg Rock and the rocky headland near the Ocean House. The sloop lay in the trough of the sea. The Professor, in spite of the seasoning of his four years' voyage round the world, and of many other cruises, began to feel internal qualms as the vessel pitched about, and presently turned in, protesting that in all his voyagings he had never experienced a more detestable specimen of the "doldrums" than that in which we now lay. I, too, for the first time in my life, felt slightly sea-sick, and also turned in.

The sloop's cabin contained four berths, two on each side. The Professor and myself took one side, the two seamen turned in on the other, while Mr. Tufts kept watch on deck, as there was some reason to fear that the sloop might drift, the only anchor we had ready for use being a small one. At midnight he was relieved by the Skipper, and with the first dawn of morning the anchor was raised, and with a light breeze the sloop slowly moved in to her moorings near the shore of Swampscott.

3

THE CUNNER   THE SCULPIN
A SCIENTIFIC SHOEMAKER

The Fourth of July morning opened with un-
wonted stillness. Nothing could be heard in the
fog but the light washing of the waves against
the sides of the sloop, and the low roar of the surf
breaking on Nahant and the rocky shore of the
mainland.

About six o'clock the Pilot arranged an iron
stove on deck, just in front of the cabin door, and
began preparations for breakfast. His first prepara-
tion, which, throughout the cruise, he never neglected, was slowly to fill and light a short black
pipe, with which stuck in his mouth, he went about
the more direct duties of getting ready the meal,
such as cutting up kindlings and bringing forth
charcoal from the dim recesses of the forepeak.

Presently he suggested that we had better have
some fish for breakfast, and directed me to bait
with clams, of which we had a pailful on board.
I reminded him that it was the Sabbath. He replied,
with due gravity, that fishing for food on the Sabbath was perfectly lawful. He would not fish for
gain or for sport on that day, but if we wanted
fish for breakfast we might take them with a clear

conscience. Perceiving this to be orthodox doctrine, I baited and dropped a line over the side, letting it go to the bottom.

In a quarter of an hour I had caught a dozen cunners, enough for breakfast. They are a species of perch, the sea-perch, but the fishermen of this region call them indifferently cunners or nippers. The dozen that I caught that morning varied greatly in size and color. They were from five to ten inches in length, and in color no two were exactly alike. The general color was black mixed with brown, with faint transverse bars of an uncertain dusky hue. One or two of the largest exhibited a light orange tint, with the head and gill-covers of a chocolate brown, and with blue fins. They are prepared for the table by stripping the skin off entirely, leaving the flesh white and delicate. I found them very good eating.

Beside the cunners, I caught a cod weighing a pound and a half, which went with them into the frying-pan. The Professor was engaged in catching jelly-fish with a hand-net, as they floated past the sloop; but, on seeing the cod, he dropped his net, baited a large hook heavily with clams, and flung it overboard. In a moment he had a bite, and, pulling vigorously, drew up a large sculpin. For the benefit of my inland readers, I will try to describe this monster, who, if his size were commensurate with his ugliness, would be the most frightful of created things. The specimen we caught was about twelve inches long, with a big, thick head, an immense mouth, great staring goggle eyes, and with about fifty spines and tubercles scattered over him, chiefly on his head.

The sculpin is a lazy rascal, and spends his time chiefly in lying on the bottom, with his fins spread, waiting till food is brought within his reach. He

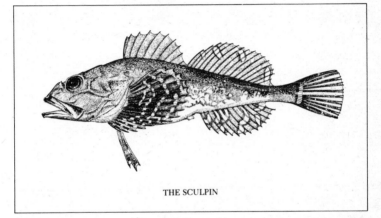

THE SCULPIN

eats everything that is edible, and will therefore bite at any bait. He is very easily caught, and comes to the surface unresistingly, gasping with his great mouth and staring with his goggle eyes. He is generally put to death, or badly hurt, before being flung back into the water, in order to keep him from biting again at the hook. On this occasion the Professor sought to induce the Pilot to cook the creature, assuring him that he would find it not bad eating. The Pilot was deaf to the suggestion, and, after knocking the sculpin's head two or three times against the side of the vessel, threw it overboard.

Our breakfast was of fried fish, boiled eggs, "hard tack" — as the sailors term crackers and biscuit, in distinction from loaf bread, which they call "soft tack" — and coffee, which we drank from large yellow mugs. After breakfast, about nine o'clock, the fog lifted.

The village of Swampscott, with its small white fishing-houses lining the shore of the shallow bay, which is no harbor, but only a barely perceptible indentation in the coast, shone out in the sunshine, backed by lovely green hills, their wooded slopes dotted by cottages and villas. Nahant, with its beaches and cliffs, crowned by its immense, fantastic-looking hotel, jutted far into the sea on our left, while to the right the surf was lazily breaking, glancing and flashing against the rocky point on which stands the Ocean House and its accompanying buildings. Behind us towered Egg Rock, with a white lighthouse perched on its narrow summit, and whiter waves foaming around its base.

We lay moored amid a fleet of picturesque fishing-vessels, about twenty in number, most of them schooners. They are called jiggers by the fishermen. The number of jiggers owned in Swampscott is twenty-five, and they are manned by upward of two hundred men. There are besides sixty or seventy dories employed in fishing, each worked by one man.

Mr. Tufts had come on board while we were at breakfast, and wishing to see his aquariums I went ashore with him in his dory. We landed on

26

a beach in front of his shop, which is almost at the water's edge, and I spent half an hour very agreeably in examining his tanks, of which he had several in fine condition. Mr. Tufts is a shoemaker, with no more education from schools than every boy in Massachusetts receives. He has educated himself by books and observation in natural history, till he has become in his specialty — marine zoology — a very intelligent naturalist. For a year or two past he has devoted himself to collecting and selling materials for stocking aquariums. To those who ordered from him he sent a keg or barrel of sea-water, and a box of two compartments — one containing the seaweed and some of the animals, the other containing the more delicate animals in a bottle or jar.

4

At 10 o'clock the anchor was raised, and with a fine breeze we got under way, bound for the south shore of Massachusetts Bay, intending to land, if possible, at Marshfield, and next at Plymouth, to take on board an artist who had agreed to meet us at that place on the 5th of July. Soon after passing Dread Ledge, the scene of numerous shipwrecks, the Professor, who was basking in the sunshine on the taffrail of the sloop, watching the jellyfish floating by, was suddenly startled by a large shark within a foot or two of his elbow. The creature was probably attracted by the sight of the Professor's red shirt, for, before starting this morning, we had discarded our shore clothes, and reduced our garments to trousers and red flannel shirts. The shark remained alongside for a minute or two, after which he was not seen again.

The wind was northwest, and the day fair and splendid, and not too warm, though it was very hot, I believe, on shore. As we passed Nahant Point we saw a great fleet of vessels coming out of Boston Harbor, spreading their white wings to fly to the uttermost ends of the earth. At 11, however, the wind shifted to the east, and the fog, which had been driven out to sea by the northwest wind, came rolling rapidly in again, involving everything in its blinding embraces. Many of the vessels returned with it, not liking to keep the sea during its continuance. For ourselves, we skirted slowly along the grim rocky barrier of Boston Harbor, with its frowning gray rocks, seamed by dikes of black basaltic trap, looking so much like hoops on a barrel as to suggest the epithet of an iron-bound shore. As the fog gained on us and grew denser, we ran in, and came to anchor between the island called the Outer Brewster and the island on which Boston Light is situated. A fog-bell near the lighthouse had been for some time sounding its dismal warning, which it continued so long as the fog lasted.

The lighthouse is a tall structure of brick, hooped with iron. "I helped to hoop it forty-eight years ago," said our Pilot. "Thomas Knox, brother of General Knox of the Revolutionary Army, was the first keeper of the light."

Our Pilot, as we called him from his knowledge of the coast, generally officiated as steersman, and always as cook. He was sixty-eight years of age, of which fifty-five years had been spent on the sea. He was still as hale, hearty, and active as most men of fifty years. His life had not been without adventure and strange vicissitudes. In 1812, when Congress declared war against England, he was on a voyage to St. Petersburg. On the return from that port his vessel was captured by an English cruiser, and he was sent a prisoner of war to Chatham, where he remained upward of a year, and was exchanged and released just before the transfer of the American captives to the fatal prison of Dartmoor. During the rest of the war he sailed from his native Marblehead in a privateer, which made a good many captures, and had three or four engagements with armed merchantmen. He continued to make long voyages for some years after peace was restored, but finally settled down into the steady pursuit of the fisheries, in the course of which he had become acquainted with almost every bay, harbor, island, headland, reef, shoal, and rock, from Cape Cod to Labrador.

Two schooners, yachts from Boston, were fishing and carousing near us, and a party from one of them was on shore on the lighthouse island, making chowder. We dined on boiled ham and corned-beef, and about the middle of the afternoon, the fog clearing away, the Skipper suggested that cunners would be good for supper, and that they could be caught close to the rocky shores of the island near which we were anchored. The Professor and myself accordingly took the dory and pulled to the nearest point of rock, on which the surf was slightly breaking. We anchored the dory as close as we could to the rocks, and, baiting with clams, dropped our lines in water ten or twelve feet deep. We caught a number of cunners, somewhat larger than those I had caught at Swampscott, two or three small cod, and as many pollack.

The pollack is a beautiful fish of a singularly elegant shape. From its agility and fine form the Bay of Fundy fishermen often call it the "sea-salmon." It is caught very freely on our shores in spring and autumn. Jeffries Ledge, which lies fifteen or sixteen miles east by north of Cape Ann, is a favorite fishing-ground for pollack, and immense quantities are taken

THE HARBOR FROM DORCHESTER HEIGHTS

there in the fall of the year by boats, which go in fleets of twenty or thirty for the purpose. Those that we caught were small, weighing about a pound and a half. Subsequently in our cruise we caught them plentifully of somewhat larger size, and frequently saw great schools of them darting out of the water.

The sky and sea were so beautiful, and the air was so delicious, the surf broke so splendidly over the many rocky points and ledges which surrounded us, that I fear we prolonged our fishing beyond what the necessities of supper strictly required. A curious whitish appearance on the summit of the huge rock near which our dory lay had attracted our attention from the sloop. As the Pilot had said that it was caused by the droppings of sea-birds, the Professor jumped ashore to examine it; instead of guano, it proved to be white quartz.

When we returned to the sloop, we found the seamen fast asleep. On awaking, and inspecting wind and tide, they decided that we must remain where we were for the present. Refreshing ourselves with lemonade concocted by the Skipper, into which he had put a little whiskey to correct the acidity, we gave ourselves up to the contemplation of a fleet of jellyfish which were sailing by in prodigious numbers. The Professor rigged a dip-net, and caught a variety of specimens.

I spent a good part of the afternoon in watching these sun-squalls, as the Skipper called them, which I think are the loveliest and the strangest of all the productions of the sea. In their delicate and fragile and evanescent beauty, I can compare them to nothing on the land except the soap-bubbles blown by a child. No one who has not seen them in their proper element can appreciate their exquisite grace. To me, one of their greatest charms was the exceeding strangeness of their forms and motions, which are wholly unlike those of any other living thing. And strangeness, as Lord Bacon long ago said, is one of the first elements of beauty. I saw, while on this cruise, I suppose a hundred thousand sun-squalls — in some places the sea swarms with them — yet I never behold one pass without a sensation of eager delight and curiosity.

About 6 o'clock the Pilot took the dory and went ashore to the lighthouse in search of milk. As he was returning from this expedition a sudden commotion in the water near the sloop attracted my attention. It occurred once or twice before I called the Professor, who was in the cabin making desperate efforts to light a cigar, the fog having affected our matches with dampness.

"A school of bluefish!" exclaimed the Professor excitedly, as his eye caught the movement to which I pointed. He shouted to the Pilot to make haste with the dory, and seized from the locker a long, stout line, at the end of which was a shining spoon-shaped piece of pewter terminated by a large hook. This apparatus is called a jig. As the dory approached he jumped in, nearly oversetting it in his hurry, and telling the Pilot to row in the direction where the bluefish last showed themselves, threw overboard the jig and rapidly unwound the line, till about thirty fathoms were trailing behind him.

Presently I saw him, standing in the stern of the boat, pull in rapidly the line. He had caught a large bluefish, which he held up for me to look at. I went below to see what the books said of the animal. Shortly afterward, hearing the Professor alongside, I went on deck. A young man, a stranger, was sitting at the oars. The old Pilot, unable to get any milk at the lighthouse, had gone ashore on the Outer Brewster, on whose green surface he had espied a cow. A young fisherman, resident there, had volunteered to row the dory while the Professor trailed for bluefish, and the Professor, after catching two or three, had run alongside to give me a chance at the sport.

The sun was just setting, and as we rowed about I forgot the bluefish in the beauty of the purple sea, of the soft, fleecy, rosy clouds, and the plashing lines of surf gently breaking over the reefs and on the rocky points of the islands. The vigorous arms of the fisherman sent the dory along at a rate that kept the jig spinning on the surface like a fish in rapid motion. Presently the bluefish broke close to it, three or four rushing at it at once, with great ferocity. A sudden jerk, a rush to the right, then to the left, a plunge, a leap, a strong, savage pull, told that a large bluefish was on the hook. I drew him in as quickly as possible, which was no slight job, for I had out at least thirty fathoms of line, and my oarsman, to whom the sport was entirely new, in his excitement kept the dory going as fast as his arms could send her.

On getting the bluefish alongside, you must lift him at once into the boat, as he will disengage himself if the line is allowed to slacken in the least. The fellow I captured was about two feet long. The jig, thrown over again quickly, was hardly out to the full length of the line before the fish were dashing at it. Several caught it in succession, and got away,

their mouths probably tearing with the powerful
tug they gave. At length one hooked himself firmly.
I pulled him in and found he was somewhat smaller
than the other. In a few minutes a third was hooked,
so large that, after hauling him in with difficulty to
the side of the dory, and seeing that he had the hook

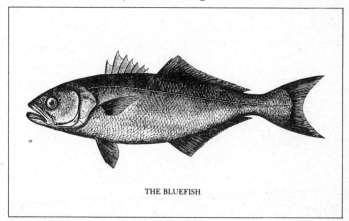

THE BLUEFISH

apparently well down his throat, I slackened the
line to give him a chance to play a little. He disengaged himself instantly and was off.

The bluefish broke water next time at some distance, and while we were rowing toward them I
saw a large fish, probably a shark, chasing them
vigorously. This put an end to our sport, for the bluefish suddenly disappeared. We saw no more of them,
though we rowed about in all directions till it grew
quite dark. Directing my oarsman to pull to the
Outer Brewster, I exchanged him for the Pilot, who
for nearly an hour had been sitting patiently on a
rock by the shore, with his pitcher of milk beside

him. The Brewster man gladly accepted two of the bluefish for his services as oarsman. As he seemed greatly enamored of the sport of catching them, we gave him a jig to enable him to follow it in the future.

The bluefish is singularly erratic in its habits. A century or two ago it was plentiful on our coast, and was held in high estimation as an article of food. During the last half of the last century and earlier years of this it disappeared entirely. Within forty years it has returned, first appearing on the coast south of Cape Cod, near Nantucket, New Bedford, and Martha's Vineyard. In course of time it made its way into Massachusetts Bay, and appears to be gradually working to the northward. Bluefish have passed Cape Ann within two or three years, though not in great numbers, and a few have been seen this year as far north as the Isles of Shoals, off Portsmouth.

The bluefish belongs to the mackerel family. The upper part of his body is of a bluish color, whence his name; the lower part of the sides and the belly are whitish or silvery.

We supped heartily on cunners and rock-cod, and at 10 o'clock turned in to sleep, the sky being cloudless and the sea calm.

5

Just at midnight we were all roused from sleep by a great crash in the cabin. Tumbling out of my berth, I found the little sloop tossing and pitching furiously. The table, which extended the whole length of the cabin, had got unfastened, and at length upset by the rolling of the vessel. The Skipper and the Pilot were already on deck, where, by the uproar, it was evident that something was going wrong. Following them I learned that the tide was setting strongly up, while a northwest wind was blowing strongly down the bay. The conflict of these two forces produced a rough sea, under the effect of which our craft was dragging her anchor and drifting toward a not very distant reef. The sky was overclouded, and the darkness was relieved only by the intermittent flashes of the revolving light. The seamen were at work forward trying to prevent the vessel from drifting, in which they at length succeeded.

I lingered awhile on deck listening to the salutes of cannon, like distant thunder, from all the surrounding shores of the bay, announcing the termination of the Sabbath and the beginning of the celebration of the Fourth of July.* The cold at length drove me below, and I turned in again, but the violent rocking of the vessel and the unusual noises prevented me from getting to sleep. By and by I rose in the darkness, put on all the coats I could lay hands upon, and groped my way to the deck. The light, as it revolved, threw over the vessel so strong a blaze that I could read the smallest print. Looking at my watch, I saw that it was just 2 o'clock. The clouds were breaking away, and the moon, like the light of the lighthouse, shone out at intervals with a fitful brilliance. The Skipper, who had been watching since midnight, uncertain if his anchor would hold, said the wind was changing; and as the vessel now drifted but little, he would turn in if I was going to stay on deck.

For two hours I stood at the companion-way, leaning over the boom, watching the black and angry waves, the flashing light, and the moon, now clouded, now unveiled, and listening to the "rote" of the sea, as our ancient Pilot always calls the sound it makes when breaking over ledges or rolling on the shore. The word is from the Latin, and I think is used by Shakespeare. It is now obsolete except among seamen.

The firing of cannon at various points on the land was audible at intervals, and now and then a fish would leap near the vessel, falling back with a

---

*The Fourth, in other words, was celebrated on July 5 that year.

great splash into the water. Occasionally I could dimly discern, through the gloom, the masts of ships that were taking advantage of the tide to glide into the harbor. They had a singularly specter-like appearance, and stalked along solemnly and silently, like the ghosts of Ossian's heroes.

It was a strange, wild scene, the most peculiar feature being the great revolving light, now throwing a ghastly glare over the vessel and the water, and a moment after subsiding into sudden darkness. I watched it with a sort of fascination till the gray light of morning began to appear, and some sea-birds on a neighboring island to twitter, and a cock to crow faintly in the distance. Shortly afterward the sun rose, and as the wind and weather were fair I roused the crew. The Skipper went ashore at the lighthouse to fill our water-firkins. The Pilot cooked the bluefish for breakfast, and in half an hour we were standing toward Plymouth with a stiff breeze from the northeast.

At 7 o'clock we passed the Lightship at Minot's Ledge, off Cohasset, the scene of many shipwrecks, and the site of the iron lighthouse, which, with its keepers, was overwhelmed by the great gale in April 1851. The lightship is a yellow two-masted vessel, strongly built and well anchored, with three or four heavy spare anchors hanging from her bow and stern, to be used in case of a gale. She had several flags flying in honor of the day.

Running down the South Shore of Massachusetts Bay, keeping generally at the distance of two miles, at a little past 10 o'clock we were off the Gurnet, a long, high promontory, stretching out from Marshfield, with two lighthouses close together on its seaward extremity, well-known to mariners as the Gurnet Lights. This high point is supposed by some antiquarians to have been discovered by the Northman, Thorwald Ericsson, who in the second summer of his sojourn in Vinland landed here, saying to his companions, "This spot is beautiful; here should I like to build myself a habitation." Being shortly afterward killed in battle with the natives, his body was buried on the promontory, which, from the crosses erected over his grave, is called in the Sagas, Krossaness, or Cross Cape.

No one on board had ever sailed into Plymouth Harbor except the old Pilot, and he but once, forty years before. The Professor, sitting on deck with the Coast Survey chart of the harbor before him, undertook to pilot us in — an undertaking not without hazard, as the bay abounds in shoals, and the channel is intricate. We got in successfully, however, and anchored just outside the sandspit which serves as a breakwater to the harbor. I believe it is thought to be the spot where the Mayflower anchored. At all events, it is the place where, five or six years ago, I got aground in a schooner attempting to sail out of Plymouth on a fishing excursion with a party of friends, and lay through a long summer's day studying the habits and manners of crabs, lobsters, and flounders, as we watched them prowling about our vessel.

The bay that forms the harbors of Plymouth and Duxbury is a broad and beautiful sheet of water, almost landlocked, with its entrance facing the east. On the north, Captain's Hill, the residence of the doughty old Puritan leader, Captain Miles Standish, rears its round, smooth summit to the height of two hundred and fifty feet, and conceals from view the

PLYMOUTH

village of Duxbury. Still farther to the north, behind other hills, lies Marshfield, the home and grave of Daniel Webster. Far to the south, fronting the Gurnet, and bounding the outer bay, the high and heavily-wooded promontory of Manomet extends for miles into the ocean. Plymouth itself is built on the slope of hills and the valleys between, and extends for about a mile along the shore, with here and there a steeple or a great elm towering above its brown roofs.

Schools of bluefish were swimming to and fro, and the Professor took the dory and tried to catch them by trailing; but they would not bite. An old fisherman, seventy years of age, who rowed his dory alongside the sloop to have a little chat with us, said he had been trying to take them all day without success. He said, also, that they had driven nearly all other fish away.

The broad surface of the bay was lively with pleasure-boats, gayly decorated with flags, and filled with young men and women. The air also was alive with flocks of black-headed terns or "mackerel gulls," as the Pilot called them, because they make their appearance in our waters about the same time that the mackerel comes. The Professor went ashore on the sand-spit near which we had anchored, to look for crabs and shells, and roused a great multitude of these gulls, who flew up, wheeling about, and uttering peculiarly shrill and painful cries. They had apparently been holding a convention on the shore, though perhaps they were only engaged in a social clam-feast over the mollusks which the waves had washed up. He saw, also, sandpipers running along the beach, diligently scrutinizing every hole which seemed likely to contain the small crustaceans which form their food. One of these crustaceans was remarkable for the height and quickness of its leaps, so high and quick, indeed, that it could scarcely be captured by the hand. A few specimens were secured by making rapid grasps at the spot where they seemed likely to alight.

Among the insects which the Professor found on this sand-spit, a race-horse beetle was conspicuous for its neat shape and bright colors. These insects must live on animal food, for there is no vegetable growth on the sands which could afford them sustenance.

But the most singular animal found on the sand-spit was a creature which the Professor said he should certainly take to be the "ant-lion," if the ant-lion had ever before been found in this country. It was an insect with a soft grub-like body and a hard beetle-like head, of a greenish color with golden reflections, and armed with a strong pair of forceps-like jaws. It had excavated a pit about an inch in depth, at the bottom of which it lay concealed, the head and powerful jaws covered by the sand. Around the margin the grains of sand were so loosely arranged that the slightest disturbance would cause them to roll down into the cavity, carrying with them into the clutches of the "ant-lion" any unlucky insect which happened to pass that way and to tread on the margin of the pit.

About sunset, the Professor and both the seamen went to the town in a dory, to mail our letters and to bring off the Artist, who was expected down by the afternoon train from Boston. Left alone in charge of the vessel, I was reading in the cabin, when I heard a shout close at hand:

"Sloop ahoy!"

I stepped on deck. A large schooner, with a numerous party of ladies and gentlemen on board, was slowly sweeping by.

"Captain, how near can we go to that p'int yon-

43

der?" said the master of the schooner, indicating with his hand the sand-spit at the entrance of the harbor.

I was so much overcome by this unexpected compliment to my nautical appearance that I inconsiderately replied, "O, quite near, quite near," as if I knew all about it. The schooner stood on. Fortunately the tide was high, and she rounded the point safely.

Late in the evening, the dory returned from Plymouth, bringing off the Artist, who, much to our surprise and pleasure, was accompanied by the Assyrian, as his friends are wont to call him, from his striking resemblance, in face and beard, to the Ninevite sculptures dug up by Layard and Botta. Their arrival completed the number we had fixed upon as desirable for the cruise, four being in fact as many as the sloop could possibly accommodate. The seamen, indeed, for the rest of the voyage slept on the cabin floor, having relinquished their berths to the newcomers.

We sat on deck for hours after supper, watching the fireworks of Plymouth, which we answered with Roman-candles and blue-lights, of which we had provided a considerable stock, not only for amusement, but to use as signals at night. The Assyrian lighted his meerschaum, the seamen their clay pipes, and the rest of us our cigars. And so we smoked and talked, nor did our conversation cease until the moonrise.

6

PROVINCETOWN
FLOUNDER
COCKTAILS

Early next morning, Tuesday, July 6, we set sail for Provincetown, Cape Cod, about twenty-five miles distant. The day must have been an excessively hot one on shore, for even on the water we found the heat oppressive, as we lay basking on deck. The wind was so light that it was some hours before we got sight of Cape Cod. As the sloop slowly glided along we gathered at the bows to watch the jellyfish floating by in countless numbers. The Skipper coiled himself up in the shadow of the sail and went to sleep. Our course was headed direct for Provincetown, whose town-house, built high on a hill and looking like a church, was visible long before the rest of the place came into sight.

Presently a slight divergence attracted my attention to our venerable Pilot. He was seated at the helm, his hand firmly grasping the tiller and his head erect, but his eyes were shut. The extreme heat had overpowered his habitual vigilance. Curiosity led me to await the result. The Professor had taken the telescope to inspect a large white object floating on the waves, which we had been for some time approaching, and which proved to be the carcass of a porpoise. The yawing of the vessel distracted his aim. He lowered the telescope, looked carefully at each end, readjusted the focus and tried it again. He caught a glimpse of the land ahead. His eye, experienced on our coast, saw that it was not Provincetown.

"Halloo!" he cried, "what does this mean? You're heading for Truro, Captain Widger."

The Pilot made no reply. He still clung to the tiller, but his chin had descended to his breast, and his honest, good-humored, weather-beaten face had disappeared under a hat that must have been the fashion at Marblehead forty years ago. The Professor surveyed for a moment the sleeping helmsman, then, while the Artist rapidly sketched his figure, took a good look at him through the telescope, and finally approached and gently tried to detach the tiller without awakening him. But though insensible to sound, the old sailor started at the first touch, however light. He shook his head to jerk his hat back to its proper position, rubbed his eyes, gave a vigorous push to the tiller, and said, with a light blush, that it was very warm, and he had been almost asleep.

"It is very hot indeed," replied the Professor, "and if you will turn in and take a nap I will take the helm. I am tired of doing nothing, and should like to steer awhile."

Captain Widger complied with the suggestion, and in half a minute was sleeping as soundly as a man could sleep. I had observed already the remarkable ease with which he went to sleep at night.

But hereafter I kept a sharp lookout for him on hot days and in plain sailing. In bad weather or in dangerous positions no pilot could be more wide awake or more trustworthy.

It was a deliciously easy, lazy voyage. We were ten hours in going twenty-five miles. To be sure, we lay-to occasionally to fish and dredge, but that did not detain us long, for we caught nothing. Either the bluefish had really driven everything else out of the bay, or we did not cast our lines in the right places. The population of the sea, like the population of the land, is fond of concentrating in favorable localities, in cities and towns as it were, leaving wide spaces desert, or at best very thinly peopled. A line dropped at random in the ocean may fall upon a finny Peking or London, or, on the other hand, upon an absolute Sahara, crossed only here and there at long intervals by scanty caravans of fish. The experienced fisherman knows the populous spots, and governs himself accordingly. But revolutions and conquests and massacres occur at the bottom of the ocean as well as on shore. The place that was once prosperous and populous decays and becomes desolate. The prototypes of Nineveh and Babylon exist in Massachusetts Bay, and it must have been their deserted precincts into which we dropped our fruitless lines. The bluefish is as cruel a devastator as the Mede or the Turk.

About half-way between Plymouth and Provincetown we dredged in water thirty fathoms deep. The bottom was soft and muddy, and yielded us some curious shells, such as are never seen upon the shore. These were remarkable for their clean, glossy appearance, bright-green color, and the comb-like teeth with which their hinge is armed. They protruded a strong, fleshy foot from between the valves of the shell, striking the hard surface of the deck in vain attempts to burrow in it as they do in the soft, muddy bottom on which they live.

About 4 p.m. we cast anchor in Provincetown harbor, which is one of the best ports in the world, easy of access, secure and large enough to shelter a thousand line-of-battle ships. It is admirably adapted by its quality and position for a great naval station. In the War of 1812 it was occupied by the British cruisers, and they could have found no point better situated from which to harass the commerce of the North. It was this harbor that the Mayflower first entered, and here, on board that vessel, was born Peregrine White, the first New Englander of European parentage.

The Professor took the dory and boarded a lobsterman who was lying-to just outside the harbor. We wanted lobsters for bait, and we wanted them for food. The Professor returned in triumph with a dozen good-sized ones, for which he had paid three cents apiece. In Boston or New York they would have cost five times as much. He brought also the important information that the harbor abounded with flounders or sand-dabs of large size, even twenty pounds in weight.

The Professor, the Artist, and I made preparations for fishing, directing the Pilot, meanwhile, to boil a lobster for supper, and to boil him thoroughly, not less than an hour. We were particular in these instructions, because by this time we had detected in the Pilot, in his capacity of cook, a proclivity to boil eggs too much and other things too little.

The Assyrian, who despised flounder-fishing, however big the flounders, said the heat made him

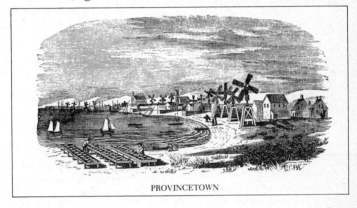

PROVINCETOWN

thirsty, and that furthermore he never ventured to eat lobster unless he had previously fortified what he called his "stom-jack" by some preventive of colic or cholera. Accordingly, while we were getting our lines and bait ready, he persuaded the Skipper to row him ashore at the town, in order that he might quench his thirst with a cocktail, or something of the sort.

When the dory returned, the Professor, the Artist, and I rowed to within a hundred yards of the shore, opposite the town, and dropped the boat's anchor in deep water. We had strong codlines, with two large hooks each, which we baited with pieces of lobster — a very difficult bait to keep on. The lines hardly reached bottom before the flounders began to bite so rapidly that they kept us actively employed in putting on bait, they took it off so easily. Nevertheless, in the course of an hour we had caught twenty or thirty, all large ones, weighing several pounds each. The largest was twenty-eight inches in length by eight in breadth. They bit so eagerly that twice we caught two at one haul of the same line.

The blowing of a horn on board the sloop announced to us that supper was ready. We wound up our lines and, rowing to the Helen, deposited our fish on the deck, giving directions to the Pilot to cook one of the flounders while we went to the town for the Assyrian, whom the Skipper said he had seen through the telescope, sitting on the edge of the wharf for the last half-hour, evidently waiting for us.

We found the Assyrian in an unsatisfied state of mind. As we rowed off, he gave us his opinion of Provincetown. The place, he said, was dry and dreary to the last degree, with a very repulsive-looking set of inhabitants. After walking about for some time, he ventured to inquire of one of the natives for a tavern. The man directed him to an edifice which bore upon its front, in large letters, the words "Union House." He entered, and was accosted by a dentist, the sole occupant, who offered to pull his teeth on moderate terms. On learning

what his visitor wanted, the dentist directed him to
a neighboring apothecary as the only man in town
who kept for sale anything to drink. The Assyrian,
in his usual confident way, demanded a cocktail. The
apothecary looked at him for some moments with
the air of a person who is too much astonished to
speak, and then replied, with grave deliberation,
"I do not know what you mean by a cocktail."

The Assyrian, in his turn, stared with astonishment. Here was a depth of ignorance hardly cred-
ible. At length he said that he wanted something to
drink. He was offered soda-water flavored, at his
choice, with lemon, strawberry, pineapple, sarsapa-
rilla. He shook his head. Was there nothing else?
"Nothing."

A bright idea flashed on the Assyrian. He described to the apothecary the method of mixing a
cocktail. The apothecary listened like one to whom
a new science is unfolded. Gradually light dawned
upon his mind. He produced, from some dusty shelf,
an almost forgotten bottle of sherry bitters. The
Assyrian seized it with alacrity. In the absence of
anything better, cocktails could be made with sherry
bitters. The other requisite materials were on board
the sloop.

Supper was ready when we got on board. We
found the flounder savory, the lobster was boiled
enough, and before turning in at nine o'clock we
drank with the Assyrian a toast to the speedy en-
lightenment of Provincetown in the knowledge of
national beverages.

7

PROVINCETOWN
THE SANDS OF CAPE COD

When we went on deck Wednesday morning, the sky was cloudless, the breeze gentle, and the long length of Provincetown, brilliant with white paint, stretched before us gleaming in the soft, warm sunshine. It is a village of three thousand inhabitants, dwelling in five or six hundred houses, nearly all of which stand on one narrow street that runs along the shore of the harbor between the water and a ridge of huge sand-hills. The Skipper took the dory and went to the town in search of "soft-tack" — loaf bread. He could not get any, and we breakfasted on hard-tack, flounders, and coffee. After breakfast we all went ashore to see the place, except the Assyrian, who protested that he had seen enough of it.

Having suffered for several days with a violent toothache, my first business was to visit the dentist of whom the Assyrian had spoken. In the search for him we discovered so many of the same profession that we were forced to form unfavorable conclusions about the teeth of the Cape-Codders. These numerous dentists, however, did not all make a living by their profession, for we found that one of them combined with it the calling of an auctioneer and of a hardware and furniture dealer. The one whom we sought was a dentist and nothing else. He did his own business well, and relieved me of my offending molar in a dexterous manner. His office apparently comprised the whole of a deserted hotel, the chief room of which, used at times for dancing, had a curious resemblance to a ship's cabin on a large scale, as befitted the maritime character of the town.

As the Professor desired to examine a beach four or five miles distant, on which the Atlantic rolls its waves unchecked by any land nearer than the "far-off bright Azores," we hired a wagon, a span of horses, and a queer little urchin of a driver, to conduct us thither over the sand-hills. In a few minutes we had left behind us the single street of the village and merged into a desert of white sand, that looked as if it had been rolled into high waves by a raging tempest, and then suddenly arrested and fixed before it had time to subside to a level. Here and there in the dells and hollows were patches of vegetation, alders, huckleberry-bushes, low pitch-pines, scrub-oaks, and clumps of wild roses, glowing with the brilliant hues which the sea air gives to flowers. But outside of the village there were no houses, fences, paths, or any traces whatever of man or beast. It was a wilderness, as it was when it first met the eyes of the Mayflower pilgrims. The horses that tugged us onward had the muscles of their rumps unusually developed from working always fetlock deep in sand.

At length we gained the shore and stood by the sea. A prodigious multitude of terns flew up at our approach, and wheeled around in the air clanging their wild and piercing cries. No other signs of life

THE SAND-HILLS

were visible, save a few white sails far away on the horizon. Signs of death were around us in the shape of fragments of wrecks thrown high on the beach by storms. I picked up a piece of bamboo which perhaps had floated from some vessel return-ing from India or China, or the isles of the East. The Professor strolled one way, and the Artist an-other, in search of specimens, and presently dis-appeared behind the curving sand-hills. The urchin of a driver busied himself commendably with bring-ing from the nearest patch of green roots a species of binding grass, which he planted here and there in the desert sand to grow and spread. More idly inclined than either of these, I sat down on a piece of wreck.

The ocean was calm, and at a distance looked like glass, but the tide was coming in, and the long lines of surf were slowly rolling up the sand with a dull, continuous roar.

> "The waves that plunged along the shore
> Said only, Dreamer, dream no more."

I turned to the little urchin who was busily transplanting roots of grass, and admiring his industry and his practical philanthropy, rose to assist him in spreading the growth of verdure for the benefit of future generations of Cape-Codders; but as I sank to the ankles in the sand after a few steps inland, contented myself with showing a proper appreciation of his labor by giving him a dime. Reseating myself, I resumed my contemplation of the sea.

> "And still the legions charged the beach,
> And rang the battle-cry, like speech;
> But changed was the imperial strain:
> It murmured, Dreamer, dream again."

The presence of the urchin plying his task with redoubled zeal disturbed and annoyed me — what business had he to be working when he might just as well be idle? — and I gave him another dime to take his wagon and horses out of sight behind a sand-hill, and continue his grass-planting somewhere else. And then, with nothing to break the spell of the sea, I sat there gazing vaguely at it until the red shirt of the Artist and the red shirt of the Professor came slowly into view, returning from their explorations.

The Professor had found nothing worth noting, and the Artist had discovered only a hut built by the Humane Society for the relief of shipwrecked persons who might make their way, cold and wet and hungry, to the shore. We mounted the wagon, the little urchin resumed the reins and drove back to the village, at the entrance to which the Artist and I got out and walked from one end of the place to the other, on a narrow plank sidewalk, examining, as we went, a number of salt-pans, and wondering at the extreme ingenuity which the inhabitants had displayed, in so varying their domestic architecture that no one of the six hundred wooden houses was like another.

The afternoon was passed in dredging the harbor and in searching for shells on the long, sandy point opposite the town; the evening in writing letters and in listening to yarns about money-digging and privateering, on both which topics the Skipper and the Pilot had respectively much to tell.

8

FROM PROVINCETOWN TO SWAMPSCOTT
MINOT'S LEDGE LIGHTHOUSE
THE SKATE

On Thursday at 8 a.m., we made sail for Swampscott, fifty miles distant as the crow flies. We were
going thither to have some alterations made in the
sloop's cabin, which would render it a little more
commodious. The day was fair, but the wind was
high and the sea very rough outside of the harbor.
The Artist, as we passed Long Point, braced himself
at the companion-way to make a sketch of the picturesque lighthouse there. Before he had finished, a
wave struck the sloop on the bows and poured over
her, drenching the sketch-book, giving the Artist a
ducking, and kicking up a bobbery among the Professor's specimen jars and bottles that sent that
gentleman rushing into the cabin in a state of high
excitement. Fortunately, not many were smashed,
and the remainder were made secure with a care
that preserved them from similar mishaps during
the rest of the cruise.

We had a splendid run, the sky cloudless, the
sea sparkling, and the wind fair and steady. As we
neared the south shore of Massachusetts Bay, the
sea grew smoother, and it was delightful to recline
on deck and listen to the cool rushing and dashing

of the water as we swept by Plymouth, Duxbury, Marshfield, and Cohasset. Now and then a hot puff of air would come from the land, reminding me strongly of Washington in that horrid hot month of June.

As we passed Cohasset we saw men at work on Minot's Ledge, building the lighthouse. Two small schooners were anchored near them. The structure is of granite, and only the foundation was yet laid, although the work was begun three years before. The rock on which it stands is of irregular form, forty-eight feet long and thirty-six feet broad, and is covered even at low tide. There are only three hours in the day when it is possible to work there, and sometimes for months together the weather is such that nothing at all can be done. In 1856, one hundred and fifty-seven hours' work was done, in 1857, one hundred and thirty hours, and in 1858, two hundred and eight hours. After the foundation was complete, however, the work went on much more rapidly. The lighthouse is a circular cone, thirty feet in diameter at the base and ninety feet high, and strengthened by large iron rods running through several courses of stone. The courses were first set up and fitted on shore and then carried off in vessels and fixed in their places.

We reached our moorings at Swampscott at 5 p.m. Our good friend Tufts, the aquarium-stocker, was on the watch for us, and soon came off with our letters and papers. While supper was getting ready, we fished from the vessel and caught cunners, cod, pollack, sculpins, and flounders, using for bait lobster and salted clams. The cod were of a beautiful red color, and weighed about two pounds each. The Pilot called them "rock-cod," and selected them for supper, throwing the rest overboard as worthless in comparison.

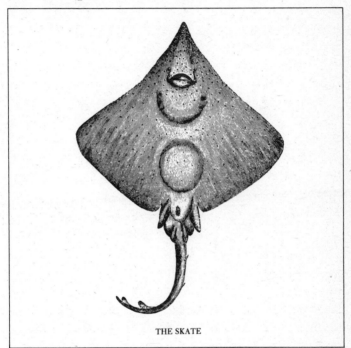

THE SKATE

I caught this evening, for the first time, a skate — a very singular-looking fish, which sometimes is found of great size, weighing as much as two hundred pounds. The one I caught weighed probably three or four pounds. It was a flat fish, with a broad, brown back, somewhat raised in the middle, the under side of the body of a dirty white. The snout was sharp and projecting, shaped like a spade; the mouth large and armed with strong teeth. It had a tail like a monkey's, long and slender, and armed with spines. There were also numerous spines upon the body. When hooked it pulled with some force, and when thrown on deck rolled itself up like a hedgehog, lashing the deck with its tail, and uttering a faint squeak as if in anger.

The peculiar form of the skate adapts it admirably to exist near the bottom. Its usual mode of progression is by a slight motion of its pectoral fins, something between flying and swimming. It is capable, apparently, of great muscular exertion. With its powerful snout it roots up clams and crushes them between its flattened teeth, which appear to act upon each other like the cylinders of a rolling-mill. It also feeds on other fish, as well as crustacea.

The young of the skate are deposited by the parent fish in their horny cases, nearly square in form. These are often found empty on the shore, and are familiarly known as "sailors' purses." As food, large quantities of the skate are consumed in London, where the flesh is considered delicate and well-flavored. It is also eaten by the French, and, I believe, is sold in the markets of Boston and New York. But our fishermen treated the creature with great disdain, and did not seem to like to have it on board. The old Pilot expressed especial disgust at the suggestion of eating it.

After supper the Skipper and the Pilot went

ashore to sleep at their own homes in the town. After their departure we lighted our cigars, and held a council of war. It was evident that the next day would be consumed by the carpenters in altering the cabin. We resolved, therefore, to spend our share of it in dredging and fishing in the vicinity, off Nahant and at Dread Ledge, the formidable roar of whose breakers was sounding in our ears. On the day after, Saturday, we would sail for Marblehead, stopping to fish on the way at certain famous shoals and ledges. Sunday we should pass at Marblehead. The rest of the week we decided should be given to Cape Ann and the Isles of Shoals. Another Sunday would find us at Portsmouth or Portland, as the wind and weather might serve, and the succeeding week would take us through Casco Bay and its hundred islands, to the lakes, and caves, and mountain peaks, and gorges of Mount Desert.

9

THE HELEN'S CABIN
DREAD LEDGE

Friday morning I awoke soon after daylight, and, by a prodigious exertion of energy, got up. I did not dress, for on board the Helen we undressed only when we bathed or when we went ashore — in which latter case, to prevent misconception, I will state that after undressing we dressed ourselves again in shore clothes. White shirts and coats we put on, only when visiting some considerable place, like Gloucester, Portsmouth, or Portland. At other places we generally went ashore in our sea rig, consisting of trousers well smeared with the slime of fish, and bleached with constant drippings and splashings of sea water, and thick red flannel shirts, one or more shirts being worn at a time, according to the weather or the fancy of the wearer. The Professor, whose ardor in pursuit of science exposed him most to the wet, generally arrayed himself in three shirts at once; the oldest in service being worn uppermost and outermost.

Getting up, as I said, soon after daylight, and giving myself a shake by way of making my toilette, I could scarcely keep from laughing as I looked around the little cabin. The Professor, whose berth was on the same side with my own, was sleeping almost in a sitting posture, his back propped up by a pillow, a greatcoat, and a huge volume of the United States Coast Guard Survey Report. He had fallen asleep while reading, for his unextinguished lamp yet burned dimly beside him, and his spectacles were still on his nose. His blanket was lying folded beneath him, and he had passed the night close to the open cabin-door, with no other protection from the cool air than his three shirts. They, however, seemed to be sufficient, for he was sleeping soundly and comfortably.

The Assyrian's berth was opposite the Professor's. An extra mattress, which the two seamen spread for themselves on the floor when they were on board, had been thrust on the top of his mattress during the day. He had neglected to remove it on turning in, and the space that was left between it and the ceiling was barely sufficient for his somewhat ample proportions. He had no pillow, and with his head thrown back and his mouth resolutely shut, he was sounding a blast with such vigor that I could almost imagine he had served as a trumpeter through all the seventeen campaigns of his famous ancestor, the mighty Temenbar. In the struggles induced by his inconvenient posture, the Assyrian had twisted his blanket around him in such fashion that, while a triple fold enveloped his body, his legs were exposed at full length, protected only by his coarse blue trousers.

The Artist, on the contrary, was lying "quiet as a stone," snugly wrapped in his blanket, which swathed him as closely as a mummy is swathed by its bandages. He had converted his portmanteau into a pillow, and was taking his sleep with a resolute expression, which said plainly that he was very comfortable, and did not mean to be disturbed.

I pinched the Assyrian's nose till he opened his mouth, which I have always found an effectual mode of checking a snorer, and went on deck to see the sun rise.

The air was mild and still, and the view superb. Before leaving us the evening before, the Skipper had purchased from a neighboring jigger a number of "hardheads," as he called them, for bait. This fish belongs to the shad and herring family, and is found in prodigious numbers all along our coast. It grows to the length of fourteen inches, and is about three inches in width. The flesh is sweet, though so full of small bones that it is seldom eaten by those who can get other fish.

The hardhead enters Massachusetts Bay about the middle of May, and remains till November. It is exclusively a sea fish, and does not, like the herring and shad, ascend the fresh-water streams. They swarm in every bay and inlet in immense schools, swimming at the surface, with their dorsal fins sticking out of the water, causing a rippling which is sometimes visible at a great distance. The shark and bluefish follow, and feed upon these schools, making such ravages among them that the gulls and other sea birds sometimes join in the chase for the purpose of picking up the fragments that have fallen from the jaws of the finny slaughterers. It is also said to be a favorite food of the great whale, who takes several hogsheads into his mouth at a time, though his gullet is so small that he can only swallow them one by one.

The common mode of taking the hardhead is by seines, many thousand being taken at a single haul. They are sold for bait to the cod and mackerel fishers, and are also used in great quantities as manure. They are spread over the land at the rate of 2,000 or 3,000 to an acre, and are ploughed or hoed in. In planting corn, a single fish is sometimes placed in each hill, to the manifest improvement of the growth of the crop. Each fish of ordinary size, weighing about a pound, is computed to be equal in richness to a shovelful of barnyard manure.

The chief value of the hardhead in Massachussetts Bay is for bait. It is in great demand among the fishermen, who use it profusely, not only by putting pieces of it on their hooks, but by grinding it up in a bait-mill and throwing it overboard by handfuls, to attract the mackerel near their vessels.

Cutting one of these fishes into small pieces with an old butcher-knife, which was always lying about on deck for that service, I baited a couple of small hooks on a cunner-line, and dropped them over the side of the sloop, more for the sake of having something in my hand as I sat on the rail looking at the scenery, than with much expectation of catching anything. In a moment I had a bite and pulled up; there were two good-sized flounders, one on each hook.

"Pretty well for a beginning," said I to myself, throwing them on the deck with a splash that evidently startled the sleepers below, for I heard some one of them muttering and rolling about in his berth. The flounders had not got the bait off, and as soon as I had disengaged them I dropped the line again. It was still sinking when I felt a bite — a stout, vigorous tug, very unlike the feeble pull of the flounder. Hauling in, I found the largest pollack we had yet caught — a handsome, lively fellow, weighing nearly four pounds. I threw him on deck with considerable emphasis, and again dropping the line, which had one bait left upon it, drew up almost instantly another pollack of about the same size.

The Professor just then stuck his head out of the companion-way, and on seeing my captures, rigged a line with his usual quickness, and for a few minutes we pulled up pollack as fast as one could wish. But in a quarter of an hour the sport was all over. For ten minutes we did not get a bite.

"This is the way with sea-fishing," said the Professor. "A small school of fish comes along and bites to your heart's content for a while. Suddenly they cease to bite, and you may fish for an hour and catch nothing."

"What can be the cause?" I asked.

"Either we have caught the whole school, or so many of them that the survivors have become cautious and have gone off, or some larger fish of another species has chased them away; or, perhaps, mere whim. Who can tell?"

The Skipper and the Pilot came on board at seven and got breakfast for us. At nine we took the dory, the Professor rowing, and went to Dread Ledge, a famous and formidable reef running out into the sea about a mile from where our vessel lay. The surf was foaming splendidly in the brilliant sunshine, over the black, savage rocks. We anchored the dory as close to them as we could with safety. Southwest of us, two or three miles distant, was Nahant, with Egg Rock rising between. Northwest was the picturesque rocky promontory on which stands the Ocean House, embowered in trees. East and south stretched the sea, dotted with the sails of the commerce of Boston.

The Professor baited two lines, and, standing up in the middle of the boat, was soon hauling in cod and pollack weighing three or four pounds apiece, much to the annoyance of the Assyrian, who was comfortably stretched out in the "arm-chair" — as the fishermen call the stern of the dory — with a cigar in his mouth, and a half-baited line in his hand. The Professor, as he quickly bent first to one side, then to the other, to pull up and throw back his lines, caused the little flat-bottomed skiff to oscillate in a way sufficiently alarming to one not used to it. The person who sits in the narrow stern always feels this oscillation most strongly. The Assyrian was evidently a little frightened. At length he said:

"I wish you would sit down, Professor, and keep still. You make the boat rock so, with your confounded jumping about, that I haven't been able to bait my line."

"Sit down! certainly, certainly," responded the Professor. "I did not observe — by George! what a bite! I've got him." And up he jumped, with a sudden spring that sent the gunwale of the dory under water, and made the startled Assyrian drop his line and clutch nervously the sides of the boat, uttering at the same time a slightly profane ejaculation.

"I beg your pardon," said the Professor, reseating himself, and taking from his hook a very lively pollack, weighing five pounds, which he threw at the Assyrian's feet, "I forgot that you wished me to sit down. Isn't that a fine fellow?"

The dory had imbibed a good deal of water in the drippings to which the Professor's activity had subjected it, and the pollack was slapping his tail on the bottom with rapid energy that spattered the face of the gentleman from Nineveh. That personage, however, said nothing, but put his heel on the tail of the fish with an emphasis that indicated considerable exasperation. He threw over his now baited hook, and in half a minute had pulled up a fine cod. Another and another followed, and in the excitement of the sport, the splashing of dirty water and the rocking of the boat were alike unheeded. He was soon almost as actively employed as the Professor himself, though he fished with a little less vigorous action.

We did not continue long the sport. We had more fish in our boat than we could possibly use, and had no desire to be guilty of wanton destruction. We stopped in time to get back to the sloop at noon, bringing with us forty-two pollack, twenty-seven cod, and a dozen cunners that weighed about a pound apiece.

10

DREDGING OFF NAHANT
MISADVENTURES
A NIGHT ROW

We found the carpenters in possession of the vessel; making cupboards and putting up racks and shelves for books, charts, clothes, and other articles. As their presence made the vessel inconveniently crowded, after dinner the Professor, the Assyrian, and the Artist got into a whaleboat belonging to Mr. Tufts and made sail for Nahant Point, intending to dredge in that neighborhood. The fishermen make great use of these boats, which are called whale-boats because in some particulars of their build they resemble the boats used in the whale fishery. They are really a convenient species of sail-boat, and generally of about five tons burden.

My companions promised to get back in time for tea, but at tea-time there was no trace of them visible. About sunset I saw them through the tele-scope far away beyond Nahant, six or seven miles distant. The breeze had died. Just before dark the whale-boat disappeared behind Nahant, and I con-cluded that my friends, finding it impossible to re-gain the sloop, had concluded to put into Nahant and pass the night there at the hotel. The Skipper and the Pilot coincided in this view, and at dark

71

went ashore to spend the night with their families, leaving me in sole charge of the vessel.

The night was exceedingly dark, and the air chilly. I confined myself, therefore, to the cabin, occupied in writing till nearly midnight, when, as I was about to turn in, I heard a distant, faint cry:

"Helen, ahoy!"

I stepped on deck, and held the light in the companion-way, so that the wind could not reach it, while its glare could be seen from without. The hail was repeated, and I recognized the strong voice of the Assyrian. But the sound came not from the direction of Nahant, but from the opposite quarter, toward the shore of the mainland. Without stopping to speculate on this phenomenon, I ran below, grasped a bunch of Roman candles, and lighting one at the lamp held it aloft, so that its fiery shower threw a momentary radiance over the sloop. I caught a glimpse of the sail-boat slowly approaching, and a shout from her crew announced their satisfaction at my signal. I lighted two more candles in succession, guided by which they got safely on board.

They were tired, wet, cold, and hungry. Fortunately the Pilot, before going on shore, had cooked a plentiful supper in the expectation that they might return before nightfall. Dry clothes proved an adequate remedy for both cold and wet. The Assyrian crawled into the forepeak, and presently emerging with two bottles of ale, proceeded to make himself comfortable in his own way. The Professor, having arranged his Coast-Survey volume for a pillow, turned into his berth, lighted his cigar, and favored me with an account of their adventures in the sail-boat.

First, they had dredged laboriously and successfully for three or four hours in the deep waters beyond Nahant, which abound in curious specimens of marine life.

Dredging, by the way, I believe I have not yet described. The implement used by naturalists is a square iron frame, like a shallow box without a bottom. It is generally about two feet square, the sides of the frame being four inches high. Below the frame, fastened to a row of holes near its lower edge, hangs a net with tolerably small meshes. A stout rope, two or three hundred feet long, is used. The dredge is dropped overboard while the boat is in motion, and is dragged along until the net-bag is supposed to be full of mud, gravel, stones, shell, and whatever else may be upon the bottom. It is then hauled up to the surface and swashed about for a few minutes to get rid, as much as possible, of the mud, which generally constitutes the chief part of its contents. Lifted upon deck, buckets, pans, basins, and other vessels are put in readiness, filled with sea-water. Handful by handful the mud is then taken from the net and thoroughly examined. Stones and other rubbish are flung overboard, but every living creature is carefully handled and washed and put into a bucket or whatever vessel may be most convenient, taking care always to immerse the animal as soon as possible into cool, fresh seawater.

On board the sailboat they had but a single bucket. Their dredging, as I said, had been successful, and at the end of three or four hours the bucket was nearly full of fine specimens. What they were the world will never know, for just as they had hauled up the last dredgeful an unlucky gust struck the vessel. There was a commotion on board, to get out of the way of the boom. The Professor's hat was knocked off by the boom, and went overboard, nearly taking his head with it. The Assyrian's long legs swung round and struck the bucket containing the specimens, the greater part of which, a minute afterward, were rapidly descending to their native depths.

Disheartened by this mishap, they gave up dredging and made sail for a fishing-bank some miles farther out to sea. They caught nothing there worth mentioning; and when it grew dark, the wind had died away. The vessel had no oars, nor anything that could be used as a paddle, except a broken pitchfork that had somehow found its way on board. With the aid of this they slowly moved onward, and, as they went, picked up a tolerably good straw hat floating by, which had doubtless fallen from some vessel. It fitted the Professor's head as well as the one he had lost.

About 9 o'clock a light breeze sprung up, and enabled them to make their way into Swampscott Bay. It was so dark, however, that they could not distinguish the sloop, and they did not learn their position till they found themselves close to the shore.

Tacking about, they stood out again, till they discerned a faint glimmer of light, which proved to come from my lamp in the cabin. They hailed it gladly, for the shore was too rough to permit a landing in the dark, and they were already suffering from cold and hunger.

11

SHROWDEN'S BANK
CATFISH   A SEA-RAVEN   A HEMDURGAN
HOPE OF HALIBUT

Saturday morning, July 10, the weather was dull and cloudy, and my companions, exhausted by the previous evening, were in no hurry to get up. At seven, the seamen came on board and got ready our breakfast, consisting mainly of the codfish we had captured the day before. The old Pilot selected three of these fish to cook, throwing the rest overboard. I noticed that he selected them with care, and without any reference to size. I asked him why he picked out those three in particular. He replied that they were the best — much the best of the lot. He could not tell why, exactly. He judged by the look — by the shape. Some cod were logy, heavy, dull; others were lively, sprightly. These last were best for food, though all cod were good eating. His explanation reminded me of the New England proverb: "All deacons are good, but there's odds in deacons."

At 8 o'clock we made sail for Shrowden's Bank, a noted fishing-place nine miles distant. We took our last look at Swampscott, whose name, by the by, is Indian, though appearently compounded of two familiar English words. It was once a favorite resort of the Indians, and was the site of one of their villages. The tribe by whom it was inhabited were called Abergonians, and at the time of the settlement of the colony they were governed by a "Squaw sachem." From 1634 to 1641 Swampscott was occupied as a farm by Sir John Humphrey, one of the original patentees of Massachusetts. For more than two centuries it was a part of Lynn. I remember it ten or twelve years ago as a small, dirty fishing-village, romantically situated, with a succession of picturesque coves, beaches, and rocky points. The summer sojourners at Nahant were fond of visiting it as a droll, queer place. Now, it is a flourishing, populous town — clean and neat, its houses resplendent with white paint, and its beaches lined with the most elegant seaside mansions in the State.

We anchored on Shrowden's Bank and began fishing with cod-lines, with a pound of lead for sinker. We baited with hardheads, and caught in a few minutes twenty or thirty codfish, averaging about three pounds weight.

The Pilot and the Skipper expected to catch halibut, which they evidently regarded as the greatest of prizes. At length I hooked something of greater size and vigor than anything we had yet taken. Observing the force with which it resisted capture, the seamen watched with eagerness its arrival at the surface, in the hope that it might be a halibut. It proved to be a catfish. It was a hideous-looking monster, thirty-two inches long by sixteen wide, weighing ten pounds. The head was large, flat on the top and blunt at the snout; the jaws filled with long, thick-pointed teeth, with which the creature snapped ferociously whenever we touched him. These jaws have great strength, and our fishermen handled their owner very cautiously. They shook their heads with marked disgust at a proposal to cook the animal for dinner; yet the flesh, when smoked, is said to have the flavor of salmon.

Half an hour afterward I hooked another cat-fish, of such size that when I attempted to lift him over the vessel's side the stout cod-line broke and he escaped.

The Assyrian, seated comfortably at the stern of the sloop, with his invariable cigar in his mouth, was lazily pulling up the occasional cod or haddock that were so accommodating as to fix themselves on his hook, when suddenly he started to his feet exclaiming, "I've got a halibut, now, I think."

We all gathered round him, as with surprising animation, he pulled in his line, of which he had out a great quantity, the tide having carried it away from the vessel. A brief observation of the process of hauling in satisfied the old Pilot. He stepped back to his own line, saying, "You've got no halibut there."

It was evidently, however, a large fish of some sort, and in time arrived at the surface. On catching sight of it the Assyrian paused, as if paralyzed with astonishment.

"What in Tophet is this?" he muttered.

"Lift it up, said the Artist, "and let us look at it."

The Assyrian reluctantly complied. It was a frightful, spinous, blood-red creature, about two feet long.

"A sea-raven," said the Professor.

The old Pilot laughed. "You may call it a sea-raven, but it's a sculpin — a deep-water sculpin."

"So it is," rejoined the Professor; "but there are many kinds of sculpin, and the books call this one the sea-raven."

The Professor then took the dory and rowed away from the sloop about one eighth of a mile, where he fished for half an hour, apparently without much success. On coming alongside he held up to

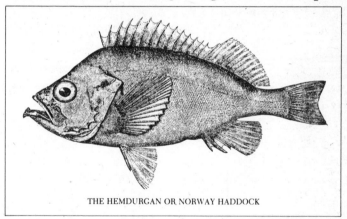

THE HEMDURGAN OR NORWAY HADDOCK

our inspection a beautiful rose-colored fish about eight inches in length.

"What do you call that?" he inquired of the Pilot.

"I call that a humdruggan."

It was a Norway haddock. It is a rare fish on our coast, and seldom eaten when taken; though on the coast of Norway, where it is caught plentifully, it is a favorite article of food, being considered a great delicacy, and eaten either cooked or dried. It is common in the seas around Newfoundland, and in the deep bays on the southern coast of Greenland it is caught in great numbers, in the way that the Professor caught it — on baited hooks attached to long lines. It has spines on the head, which the Greenlanders formerly used for needles.

The Pilot and the Skipper both expressed a good deal of dread of this handsome and apparently harmless fish. They considered the spine poisonous, and the Skipper related several instances in which he had known persons to be dangerously wounded by handling it. The Professor pooh-poohed at these stories, though it was possible, he said, that a wound made by the spines of the fish might become badly inflamed, as often was the case with wounds made by the claws of a cat or the teeth of a rat.

The Artist, who was fishing from the side of the vessel, now called out that he had got a halibut. The old Pilot took hold of his line, and after pulling for a moment his countenance lightened up and he exclaimed exultingly: "A halibut, and a big one too! Now, gentlemen, you'll see some sport. Now you'll see what fishing is. Let me manage him!"

Rapidly, but continuously, he pulled on the line for a few moments, holding it so that a sudden rush of the huge fish would not meet with sufficient resistance to break the cord. We held our breath, and gathered round to watch the struggle which was to ensue when the halibut put forth his strength. But no struggle came. The Pilot pulled and pulled with greater difficulty, till it was evident that the line would bear no more strain. He then paused, and fingered it a little, gave a jerk or two, dropped it suddenly as if it burned his fingers, uttered a low whistle, and walked to his own line, which he began to pull in slowly with a chapfallen expression.

"What's the matter?" inquired the Artist.

"Why don't you pull up the halibut?"

"Halibut be hanged!" responded the old man; "your line is foul of a cable which somebody has lost here."

The Artist pulled stoutly and the line broke, coming up minus the hooks. He protested, however, that he had at first something living on the line, which had probably got away in consequence of coming in contact with the sunken cable.

12

Sunday morning in the picturesque harbor of Marblehead was as lovely as sunshine and sea and scenery could make it. As the day advanced, the heat became oppressive. On shore, we afterward learned, it was the hottest day of the year — the mercury rising in some instances above 100°.

Toward noon we got into the dory and, with the Pilot for oarsman, rowed across the harbor to the narrow peninsula which separates it from the ocean. Leaving him in charge of the boat, we walked across the field half a mile or so, till we found ourselves on the ocean shore. It is a bold, rocky coast, indented with many little coves, with tiny sandy or gravelly beaches. Selecting the prettiest and shadiest of these recesses, we cooled off with a long, luxurious bath. Strolling then to a headland, crowned by a group of stately elms, we sat down in their shade on the grass, lighted our cigars, and refreshed our eyes with the contemplation of a scene of blended land and water, promontory and inlet, hill and meadow, cultivation and wildness, that southward has no rival nearer than the bay of Rio Janeiro, and northward is not surpassed in natural beauty till you reach Mount Desert.

Certain interior sensations, symptoms of the approach of the dinner hour, at length caused us to turn our steps toward the Helen. Crossing the Neck, we found the dory where we had left it on the beach, but the Pilot had disappeared. We hunted for him up and down the shore, in caves, behind rocks, under bushes — everywhere. He was not to be found. He had obviously vanished. We had no resource but to await his reappearance. To sit or stand in the fierce sunshine, which poured down upon the boat, was out of the question. Descrying a barn at some distance we went to it for shelter, and discovered our missing Pilot stretched upon a heap of hay fast asleep. He, too, had prudently retreated from the fervor of the sun, and yielded himself to his usual tendency to sleep when there was nothing else to do. Rousing him, we rowed back to our vessel, and after dinner, the heat having grown still more oppressive, we turned in and went to sleep ourselves.

Our slumbers were not of long duration. They were cut short by a tremendous peal of thunder. We arose and went on deck.

When we went below not a cloud marred the serene blueness overhead, not a breath of wind disturbed the fervid, glowing atmosphere, or mitigated the fierce heat; but now the heavens were shrouded with a pall broken only by flashes of lightning, while furious gusts swept madly over the harbor, lashing the waters into short, sharp waves, crested with foam. It was the most formidable thunderstorm ever known in the annals of New England. It raged, I believe, over the whole of Massachusetts. In Cambridge alone the lightning struck in more than forty places, through that city, its peculiar position, is usually remarkably exempt from the influence of thunderstorms.

The temperature lowered very rapidly. There was a gust of rain, and then suddenly we were engulfed in a dense fog, which, however, did not rise high above the surface of the water; for I was struck by the strange appearance in the air of the topmasts of the surrounding vessels, while their hulls were entirely hidden. Gradually the fog turned into rain, and by nightfall the weather was so cold that we went to bed at dark to keep ourselves warm. The wind was northeast, and blowing pretty hard, and I noticed, before turning in, that the Skipper and the Pilot were busy rigging a large anchor which we had on deck, but which we had not yet had occasion to use. They predicted that the wind would increase in the night, and, as it was blowing directly into the harbor, we should be likely to need an additional anchor. The old Pilot said that he remembered a northeast storm, many years ago, in which every vessel in the harbor was driven ashore.

The prediction of the seamen was verified. About midnight we were roused by an outcry on deck, and, turning out, found that the wind was blowing almost a gale, and that the sloop, in spite of her additional anchor, was drifting under the impulse of wind and waves directly upon the great black rock which rose from the water a hundred yards southwest of us. She drifted slowly, and we watched her progress with some anxiety. Fortunately, when we were about fifty yards from the frowning rock, our anchors caught in the moorings of another vessel and arrested our dangerous progress.

MARBLEHEAD

The next morning, Monday, was so cold and damp that the seamen dragged forth a small stove from the forepeak, and made a fire in the cabin. We went ashore to take a look at the town, which has always been reputed one of the queerest places in New England. It was settled before 1645, and is built on a high, rocky, irregular peninsula about four miles in length and two in breadth. The streets are narrow, and are laid out on the pattern of the paths in a modern landscape garden, with a careful avoidance of straight lines. We saw few of the inhabitants, and most of those we saw were small boys, who had a weather-beaten look and sported pea-jackets and top-boots. The people were formerly the most uncivilized in New England, and the boys so rude and turbulent as to be a terror to strangers, whom they were accustomed to stone, or, as they themselves expressed it, to "rock," for amusement. But of late years the place has much improved.

After dinner we made sail for Gloucester. The wind having abated, our progress was very slow, and about the middle of the afternoon we lay to and fished. Half a dozen rock-cod were hauled up in a few minutes, and the Pilot, having nothing else to do, began to prepare them for the frying pan. As he cleaned them, he threw overboard the entrails, which floated for a while on the surface.

Almost instantly a flock of stormy petrels, or Mother Carey's chickens as the sailors call them, gathered round the garbage. A moment before but one of these birds was visable. They were very bold, coming close alongside of the vessel, and seizing pieces of the floating prey larger than themselves, with which they would strive to fly away. Sometimes two of them would take hold at the same time of the same piece, and tug in opposite directions. The Professor seized his dip-net, and stationing himself at the side of the vessel, directed the Pilot to throw over a handful of garbage so close that it would float within reach. The birds gathered round, and the

Professor, with his usual adroitness, captured in succession half a dozen of them. They were so greedy and bold that he might, if he had pleased, have taken the whole flock.

In taking them from the dip-net and throwing them on deck near the companion-way, they showed remarkable stupidity, or inability to walk on anything but water. They dashed about under the bench which surrounded the small standing-place for the helmsman, in front of the cabin, knocking their heads against the under surface of the bench as blindly as a bird or insect will knock against the glass of a half-opened window, instead of flying out of the aperture. In no case did one of them succeed in getting clear of the deck without our assistance. When liberated, I noticed that they all flew away in the same direction until they were out of sight.

The last one that we caught the artist took into the cabin to make a drawing of it. It was very tame, and remained for a quarter of an hour without struggling, loosely held in the hand until its portrait was secured, when it was permitted to rejoin its companions. Like all those we captured, it had a singularly gentle and innocent expression, and its resemblance in this respect to a young chicken was so great that we were satisfied of the appropriateness of the term chicken commonly applied to the birds by sailors — though why it should be called Mother Carey's is an unsolved mystery.

A flock of these birds will sometimes follow a

vessel for months together. They sleep on the water at night, and catch up with the ship in the morning, guided in their search for it perhaps by instinct, perhaps by the small floating substances, such as scraps of food, which their keen eyes can detect in its wake. The Professor told us that he had frequently caught them in the Pacific Ocean, and let them go again

GLOUCESTER HARBOR

with a colored thread tied to their legs. One individual, thus marked, followed the ship for six weeks, and was seen every day. It has been a question much discussed among naturalists where and how this bird breeds. But at Grand Manan the Professor found their nests in immense numbers. They burrow, like the cliff swallow, in cliffs of sand. There are cliffs at Grand Manan so perforated by them as to resemble gigantic honeycombs, around which they

88

swarm in multitudes so prodigious as almost to blacken the air.

About sunset we cast anchor in Gloucester harbor. The weather was thick, and the wind very light. As we slowly made our way in, the Skipper noticed a small schooner, a fishing jigger from his own town of Swampscott, which was also creeping along with the tide. It was owned, he told us, by a neighbor of his, and was manned by two men, one of whom was known in Swampscott by the nickname of "Cousin," who, he said was a very merry fellow, and would amuse us by his droll remarks. We accordingly stood toward the jigger, and when near enough for conversation, hailed it.

Cousin was at the helm, and in anything but a jolly mood. In answer to our inquiry for news, he replied that he had "lost his skipper."

"Lost his skipper!" exclaimed the Assyrian; "what does the man mean? I never heard before of losing a skipper: the fellow must be joking."

But I observed that the faces of our Swampscott fishermen grew grave on hearing Cousin's unexpected reply. They were too familiar with the dangers of their vocation to be much perplexed by the strange catastrophe that had befallen their neighbor. The old Pilot silently relinquished the helm to the Professor, and he and the Skipper took the dory and went aboard the jigger. They returned in a few minutes, and confirmed Cousin's statement. He had really "lost his skipper."

The two men had been sent to some distant

fishing-bank, and on their return, while yet out of sight of land, had been overtaken by night. They kept watch, one at a time. The first half of the night was Cousin's watch. At midnight he roused his companion, who took the helm, while Cousin turned in to sleep. In the morning when he awoke the skipper was missing — gone — vanished. Not a trace of him was visible. The little schooner was easily searched — he was not on board. The dory stilled towed at the stern — he had not gone off in that. The inevitable conclusion was, that he had somehow fallen overboard, and been drowned. But how, when, or why, were questions that would have baffled forever all the coroners of the Commonwealth. After looking in all manner of impossible places for his missing comrade, Cousin, with a heavy heart, steered for Cape Ann, the nearest land, to report his loss and take counsel with the friends and neighbors whom he knew he should meet in Gloucester harbor, which is the great rendezvous of the Massachusetts fishermen.

Our Pilot and Skipper, who knew both the men intimately, expressed the most entire confidence in the accuracy of Cousin's statement. His companion had probably fallen overboard in a fit or by a careless misstep in the dark, and, like many of the fishermen, being unable to swim, had gone down unseen and unheard. They showed evident concern for their neighbor, but still could not repress a certain degree of amusement as they thought of Cousin's astounding bewilderment on getting up in the morning and finding that he had lost his skipper. They had been so much in the habit of laughing at, or laughing with him, that a touch of the ludicrous could not but mix itself with even so grave and shocking an event.

On our way up to the harbor we had dressed ourselves in shore-clothes, and immediately on casting anchor we went ashore and made our way to the Gloucester House, where we ordered supper. While that was getting ready, we strolled out into the narrow, winding streets, which were thronged by sailors and fishermen, of whom there are sometimes three or four thousand in port at once. Supper being ready at 9 p.m., we sat down and made a night of it, with appetites rendered keen by ten days' abstinence from the forms, food, and appurtenances of civilized life. It was pleasant to see a tablecloth once more, to sit in a chair, and to eat something beside fish and salt meat. We lodged that night at the hotel, and it was really delightful to turn in without trousers to a bed broad enough to roll about on.

13

The next day there was little or no wind, and not
a vessel left port. We amused ourselves, therefore,
with walking about the town during the forenoon,
visiting the Pavilion, a fine hotel on the edge of the
harbor, near to which are the ruins of an old fort,
commanding a fine prospect, where we basked for
an hour or two in the sunshine, watching the mack-
erel-fishers in the harbor. We dined at the hotel,
and after dinner went on board the sloop and resumed our sea-rig.

In the evening we received visits from several
Swampscott skippers, whose vessels, like our own,
were wind-bound in the port. One of these men sat
with us till midnight, spinning the most monstrous
and incredible yarns, which he narrated with a serene gravity that would almost have persuaded
the hearer to believe any lie. He was a marine Mun-
chausen of the first water, and his adventures were
nearly as wonderful as those of the renowned Baron
himself.

You could mention no island that he had not
visited, from Borneo and Madagascar down to No

Man's Land, or Pitcairn, or the Isle Royale of Lake Superior. He had sailed on all seas except the Polar Sea, and that he reluctantly admitted he had only seen at a distance. He had conversed with all potentates, from the Czar Nicholas to the King of the Cannibal Islands, and kindly gave us each a couple of cigars, which he said were from a box presented to him by his friend the Captain-General of Cuba, a very choice and rare brand that could not be got for any money even in Havana. The last part of this assertion was probably true. No such cigars were ever seen in Cuba, for they were obviously of Connecticut tobacco, and we had ourselves bought some of the same choice kind at a shop in the main street of Gloucester for two cents apiece.

We spoke of snakes. On this topic he spread himself amazingly. He had often seen the sea-serpent, and once when cruising for swordfish off Nantucket, had harpooned the monster from the deck of his vessel, and had been towed out to sea a hundred miles in thirty minutes, when the line broke and the creature got away.

"But speaking of snakes," said the visitor, lighting one of the Captain-General's Havanas with much deliberation, evidently to gain time for invention, "if you want to see snakes you must go to the East Indies. I was once lying at anchor in a little port on the coast of Sumatra, waiting for a cargo of pepper. The weather was intensely hot, and we left all the hatches open at night. I got up early one morning and found the gunwales of the ship nearly down to the water's edge. Supposing that we had somehow sprung a leak and were sinking, I roused up the men and sent a couple of them down the main hatchway to see what the matter was. They did not come back, and after waiting a few minutes I sent the mate, who looked in cautiously with a lantern, and reported that there was a serpent in the hold, and that he had probably swallowed both the seamen, as the feet of one of them were sticking out of his mouth. From the depth to which his weight had sunk the ship he was evidently a big one. Prompt measures were necessary. I directed the men to rig a tackle and fall, and let down a stout rope with a running noose right over the hatchway. I then mustered all our fire-arms and gave the snake a volley to rouse him. He soon reared his head out of the hold, I dropped the noose over it, the men ran him up, while the mate and I with axes chopped him in two. He was so long, sir, that it took the whole forenoon to haul him out by sections, cut him up, and throw the pieces overboard."

*   *   *   *

Wednesday, July 14, there was a fog in the morning, but not a very dense one, and we had grown so tired of inaction that we rigged a pair of oars, and about 9 a.m. began to sweep the sloop out of the harbor — a slow and toilsome process, but successful in time. We passed languidly by the villas that line the shores of the harbor, passed the light-houses, passed the reef of Norman's Woe, the scene of Longfellow's ballad:

NORMAN'S WOE

"Such was the wreck of the Hesperus,
In the midnight and the snow!
Christ save us all from a death like this,
On the reef of Norman's Woe!"

Great schools of hardheads were rippling the
water all around us. A light breeze at length sprang
up, and we laid our course for Rockport, on the
outside of Cape Ann. Off Thatcher's Island, at the
extreme end of the Cape, we encountered a
fleet of large sloops laden with granite from Rockport, which they were taking to Boston. They were
very deeply laden, and as they rolled along they
dipped a volume of water which immediately poured out again in great streams from their scuppers.
There was a heavy swell on the sea, and the water
had a strange metallic lustre like that of blue steel.
We had a slow, dull breeze, and the tide was

95

against us. We did not advance, on an average, more than a mile an hour, and at times actually retrograded.

We were nine hours in going nine miles. Gradually the swell subsided, and the sea grew very smooth, with a gray leaden hue. Flocks of terns were wheeling and screaming overhead, and schools of pollack leaping all around us.

When within a mile of Rockport, as we coasted slowly along, at no great distance from the high, rugged shore, we discerned among the fissures in the rocks a cavity of unusual size which greatly attracted our curiosity. The Professor and I took the dory and rowed into it; not without difficulty, notwithstanding the usual smoothness of the sea. It proved to be a high narrow cavern, extending about a hundred feet into the rock. We named it Helen's Grotto in honor of the sloop. On emerging from it we found the vessel had kept on her way, instead of lying to for us, and was already at the entrance of Rockport harbor. We accordingly had to row after her, and as the tide was against us did not overtake her till she came to anchor in the middle of this curious little port, which is partly artificial, and will shelter fifty or sixty small vessels.

We made our supper on cunners, which we caught from the side of the vessel, and on bread, for which we sent one of the men ashore, and went to bed at 9 o'clock, a dark fog covering the water and giving us a poor prospect for a rapid voyage tomorrow.

14

The town of Rockport is declared by the Gazetteer of Hayward to lie four miles northeast from Gloucester Harbor, thirty-six northeast from Boston, and eighteen northeast from Salem. It comprises all the seaward portion of the extremity of Cape Ann, and from the settlement of New England to the present time, the men of Rockport have been distinguished for their enterprise in the fisheries, "thereby," as Hayward judiciously remarks, "rendering them serviceable to their country abroad, and fit companions for its intelligent and rosy-cheeked damsels at home."

We saw but little of the town. The fog was so dense that we could only discern that we were in a small harbor, partly artificial, with a huge mole of granite between us and the ocean. There were fifteen or twenty schooners in the port which afforded room for perhaps twice as many more.

The Artist and I got the Skipper to row us ashore before breakfast next day, July 15. We landed on a dirty beach, covered with the decaying offal of fish, the stench of which was almost suffocating. A narrow street led us to the center of a large and prosperous-looking village, where we mailed our letters and made some purchases, especially of "soft tack," of which we bought a quantity that caused the baker to stare and gasp with amazement. We knew we should be likely to get none for several days, and had found by experience that six healthy men, with sea appetites, could consume an enormous amount of bread.

ROCKPORT

When we got on board again we found the Professor and the Assyrian in a state of deep disgust at the smell of rotten fish which filled the air, and which, indeed, had been so disagreeable on the previous evening that we should have hoisted anchor and gone outside of the harbor to pass the night on the open sea, had not the fog been so thick that we could not see our vessel's length ahead of us. It was so unpleasant on deck that, immediately after supper, we had lighted our cigars and closed the cabin doors, to smother with the fumes of tobacco the fishy odors from the shore.

As soon, therefore, as breakfast was over, we raised the anchor, rigged the oars, and rowed our little vessel out of the port, just as so many Greeks would have done three thousand years ago. I have been amused during the whole of this cruise with its resemblance to the style in which the ancients made their voyages. The Helen, I suppose, could not be much smaller than the bark which carried her namesake, the faithless wife of Menelaus, from Sparta to Troy. And though we did not, like the Greeks of that age, haul our vessel on shore at night, we ran regularly into port as the darkness approached, and never ventured far from land. The coast of New England, north of Boston, with its inlets and islands and rocky headlands and frequent harbors, is not unlike the coast of Greece.

The fog was still as dense as ever, and when we had got half a mile or so outside the harbor we ceased rowing and let the vessel drift. The Professor, taking a couple of cod-lines, got into the dory and rowd away from the vessel. In two minutes he was out of sight, and presently the sound of his oars became inaudible. The tide was drifting us away from the land, and we soon grew anxious for the safety of our companion. In such a fog, without a compass, the Professor, after a few turns round would have found it as difficult to make the land as to find the sloop.

The Skipper, who was seriously alarmed, took the horn and sounded a sonorous blast. It was presently answered by a blast from the land. All along the coast, as far north as population extends, even to Labrador, the humane and kindly custom prevails of blowing a horn in time of fog as a guide to the mariner. Such a signal from a vessel, anywhere from Cape Ann to Labrador, will be promptly responded to from the shore, if the shore is inhabited. We blew again at intervals of five minutes to guide the Professor. By and by we heard the sound of oars, and that gentleman came alongside, having caught nothing but a lobster, which he had somehow contrived to entice into his dory.

He seemed in no hurry to come on board, but asked the Skipper to give him a cup of water, a piece of bread, and half a dozen cigars. He then said to me —

"You are always interested in cunner-fishing, Carter. Jump into the dory and come along, and I will show you the king of the cunners. But first light a cigar, and take a couple of lines from that locker. There — give me a light — and take the oars, if you please."

I pulled toward the shore, while the Professor lighted another cigar and baited the lines with the flesh of the lobster he had taken. The fog was so dense that the shore was not visible until we were close upon it. We anchored the dory in water ten or twelve feet deep, at the distance of as many yards from the high rocks, black and slimy with seaweed, that line all that part of the coast of Cape Ann. The sea was as smooth as glass, and the water so clear that the smallest objects on the bottom were distinctly seen. Directly beneath our boat, and for a few feet on every side, the bottom was clean sand, free from weeds. But this clear space, which was about twenty feet in diameter, was surrounded by heaps of rocks which rose to within three or four feet of the surface. Around the bases of these rocks, and in their crevices, grew a dense thicket of marine plants, making a vegetable ring about the rocks two or three feet wide.

"Here is where I caught the lobster," said the Professor, "and with patience and dexterity we can catch enough of them to keep us supplied with food and bait for the rest of the week. Did you ever see so many cunners before? Look sharp, and you will see a very large one."

The water beneath us, indeed, swarmed with cunners of all sizes and all colors. There were some not larger than a man's finger, and others that appeared upward of a foot in length. Most of them were blackish in hue, but there were several of lighter colors, and one or two of a bright orange tint. There must have been hundreds of them in sight at once. They swam about slowly and lazily, sometimes hiding in the thickets of sea-weed, then gliding out and cruising vaguely round, apparently without any definite object.

I lowered a baited line from the side of the boat. In a moment it was surrounded by a crowd of eager fishes, their apathy gone, and their tails wagging with excitement. I now saw an explanation of a phenomenon that had often puzzled me while fishing for cunners in water so deep or turbid that the fish, until caught, were not visible. While so fishing, you frequently have a smart, bold bite, and your line is carried off for a yard or two with a rush that makes you feel sure you have caught a biter. But with such a bite you seldom, if ever, take a cunner. The reason is, as I now saw, that it is only the smallest cunners that bite in that fashion. Little fellows, not yet arrived at years of discretion, will imprudently thrust themselves in among a crowd of larger and wiser fish, who are gravely contemplating the bait before venturing to touch it, and suddenly snapping hold of a corner of it, a young gentleman will drag the tempting morsel away from under the very noses of his seniors. He seldom runs with it more than two or three feet, however, then drops it, and scuds off as fast as his tail will carry him. The larger cunner, if he takes the bait at all, takes it soberly and considerately, and does not make a greedy snatch at it. He is very expert at getting the bait off without being caught by the hook.

I was so much pleased with watching the movements of the cunners that I did not care to catch them. I had taken five or six of moderate size, who hooked themselves in spite of my endeavors to prevent it, and had exhausted my share of the bait, when the Professor, who had been pulling them up in considerable numbers, called out to me from the other end of the dory:

"There is the king of the cunners I told you of. He is just coming round that point of rock. Did you ever see a bigger one?"

It was, indeed, a large one — by far the largest cunner I had ever seen. His great comparative size was apparent when he moved in a throng of his own species, as he did presently, sauntering about for a few minutes with a stately air, brushing aside his subjects with a majestic sweep of his tail. After promenading for a short time without finding anything worthy of his royal attention, he glided slowly into the recesses of a patch of seaweed at the base of one of the rocky heaps. Not doubting that he would soon reappear, I determined to capture him. I cut off the head of a small cunner and fixed it securely on the hook. The common herd of cunners attacked this bait as soon as it was dropped among them, but could make nothing of it. They could not disengage it nor gorge it, and it was so hard they could make little impression by nibbling. Still, they tugged and pulled and pushed, till nearly all had tried their teeth upon it. Not one, however, could take it in.

At length the big one came out of his lurking place among the sea-weed, where probably he had been feeding upon crustacea. As he lounged about, I brought my bait several times in front of his nose. Again and again he poked it away with disdain. At length, suddenly it seemed to strike him as something that demanded attention. He paused before it for about a minute, evidently considering what it meant as it hung within an inch of his nose, wagging his tail gently all the while to keep himself in position. I felt sure he would take it; but no; with one sweep of his tale he wheeled about and darted away toward the rocks.

"He is gone," said I to the Professor, who was watching the affair with interest.

"No, there he comes again; he has thought better of it."

The cunner had got his nose among the seaweeds, when he paused, wheeled again, made a straight line for the bait, took it in his mouth without the slightest hesitation, and deliberately marched off with it to his den in he rocks. He did not rush off as a young cunner would have done, but moved away with a grave unconcern, that said as plainly as words could say it: "I know what I am about. I have fully considered this matter, and it's all right. This prize is mine, and I'm going to enjoy it at leisure."

I gave him plenty of slack line, and when he had gotten fairly housed in his place of refuge, I slowly counted a hundred before I ventured to pull him up. The bait was so large and tough that I doubted whether he would swallow it. When he carried it off, he merely took hold of it with his thick, fleshy lips. At length I pulled. I had him. He had fairly swallowed the bait, and was fast enough. I had a measuring line in my pocket, and found his length was sixteen inches. His weight I cannot tell, for we neglected to weigh him after our return to the sloop.

A few minutes later we heard the sound of a horn from the direction in which we judged the Helen to have drifted, though at a considerable distance.

"They want us to come back," said I; "what can the matter be?"

The Professor made no reply for a moment, but attentively scanned the neighboring shore, as if he were considering the state of the tide. At length he spoke.

"What time is it? I have left my watch hanging in the cabin."

"So is mine. I haven't the least idea of the time. In this fog, all hours of daylight seem pretty much alike."

"As well as I can judge by the tide," said the Professor, "it is considerably past noon. I have smoked three cigars, which ought to have taken three hours, and it was after ten when we set out. I suppose they want us to come to dinner; but I've no notion of going back without a lobster or two for supper. What say you?"

"Agreed. Hand me a bit of that bread, and I'll stay till dark if you wish."

Two or three short blasts on the horn, in rapid succession, indicated that our comrades were getting impatient.

"Let them toot," said the Professor; "it will do their lungs good. Besides, they deserve to be worried a little for making us row so far yesterday. Now for a lobster."

Being a good deal puzzled how he expected to catch lobsters with a hook, I watched his proceedings with attention. While fishing for cunners I had observed several lobsters prowling about, backing in and out from the seaweed and scattering the cunners by their approach. Two or three small flounders had also made their appearance, sliding along on the bottom, taking my bait with their usual stupid greediness and getting caught accordingly. The Professor cut a piece from one of these, fastened both the hooks of his line in it and dropped it over the side of the dory. It was instantly surrounded by a crowd of cunners. By gently jerking the line up and down he kept these from stealing the bait, and in a few minutes a lobster darted out of the seaweed, and rushing among the crowd as if to see what was going on, put them to flight. He did not seem to notice the bait himself, but the Professor, following his movements, dropped the tempting morsel in front of his claws. Presently he seized it with avidity and conveyed it to his mouth. The Professor let him have it for a minute until his claws were somewhat entangled in the line, and then slowly and gently pulled him up till his horns or feelers appeared above the water. Seizing these the Professor drew the lobster into the boat. The instant the creature felt his touch it disengaged itself from the line.

"The hook is of no use," remarked the Professor. "I have caught them this way with merely a piece of fish tied to the end of a string. All that is needed is quickness and caution. The lobster will let you draw him to the surface if you do it quietly so as not to alarm him, but if he is frightened in the least he is off like a flash. You must grab him the instant his horns are out of the water."

I baited my line with a piece of flounder, and watched for a long time in vain. Only one lobster showed himself, a small one which the Professor caught. I was nearly out of patience when the Professor, who was watching his line on the opposite side of the boat, said: "Here is the father of the family, probably just waked up from an after-dinner nap. He is under the boat; look out for him. I shall leave him to you."

The hard-shell gentleman thus designated soon appeared on my side of the dory. He was truly a large one, and hideous to look at. For a good while he would pay no attention to my bait, but amused himself with chasing the cunners, who sculled out of his way with an alacrity that indicated no small degree of terror. At length I contrived to attract his notice by dropping my sinker on his head. He seized the bait promptly, with a sort of clumsy wrath, and conveyed it to his mouth. I pulled him up gently an inch or two at a time till his horns were within my reach.

"Grab him!" said the Professor, who had watched the proceeding anxiously.

It was easier said than done. I put out my hand to take him by the horns, but with so much reluctance to run the risk of an encounter with his formidable claws, that before I had secured him he let go the line and sank to the bottom.

"Bah!" exclaimed the Professor, "you have lost him. Was that cowardice or only clumsiness?"

"A little of both," I replied; "but you must recollect that I am not accustomed to handle lobsters, whereas you have been intimate with the crab tribe ever since you were out of your cradle."

I tried again, and being less nervous, succeeded in getting the big lobster to the surface and lifting him into the boat. We caught three more, and concluded we had enough for all reasonable wants. We accordingly pulled up the anchor and the Professor, who hated rowing, sculled the dory slowly out to sea in the direction from which we last heard the sound of the horn. We soon lost sight of the land, and could see nothing of the sloop. Presently, however, we heard someone singing, and in a few minutes the tall mast of the Helen loomed through the fog. In another minute we could see her deck, but no one was visible upon it. Motioning me to be silent, the Professor slowly and noiselessly impelled the dory toward the vessel's bows. The singing continued, and we perceived that it came from the Assyrian, who was lying in a coil of rope on the deck, with his face toward the sky, instead of watching the horizon as he ought to have done.

We were now close aboard the sloop, and the Professor, putting his hand to his mouth, shouted through it, in the gruffest tones he could command, an unintelligible order to the sloop to get out of his way or he would run her down. The startled Assyrian sprang to his feet with an alacrity that showed how imminent he thought the danger. Evidently he expected to see a vessel of at least a hundred tons bearing down upon him through the fog.

"You keep a bright lookout here," said the Professor, as we stepped aboard.

"You have given a great shock to my nerves," said the Assyrian. "But I forgive you, in consideration of your safe return. We have been really anxious about you, my dear fellow, and have had thought of alarming the coast and turning out a dozen steamboats in search. As it is, we have rowed this infernal galley up and down and round and round till we are all beat out. Where on earth have you been hiding?"

"Is dinner ready?" inquired the Professor, wholly unmoved by the Assyrian's distresses.

"Dinner! What time do you think it is?"

"About three, perhaps four," said the Professor.

It was nearly seven. They had had a dismal day on board the sloop — had seen nothing, caught nothing, and done nothing but eat and sleep.

As night was fast approaching, and we were resolved not to return to Rockport, we had no alternative but to pull for Pigeon Cove Harbor, about two miles distant. We reached there, by hard rowing, just about dark.

PIGEON COVE

15

The little harbor of Pigeon Cove, where we anchored about dark on Thursday, July 15, is like the neighboring harbor of Rockport, partly artificial, being protected from the ocean by a high granite wall. It was filled with vessels, mostly fishing schooners, of from fifty to a hundred tons, manned each by ten or twelve men. They had taken refuge here from the fog, and were waiting impatiently for a breath of wind to enable them to get away. Most of them were from Gloucester and Swampscott, though there were a few from the South Shore and one or two from Provincetown.

While we were rowing the vessel into port, the Pilot had boiled the big lobster and made tea. So we had supper immediately on coming to anchor. After supper the Assyrian, protesting that in consideration of the fog, the lobster, and hard work at the oar, our "stom-jacks" deserved a little something to strengthen them, volunteered to concoct a general cocktail. He produced his bottle of strong bitters, which he kept carefully tucked away in a corner of his berth. It was nearly empty. Still there was enough to lay the foundation of a cocktail in each

111

of the six tumblers, which stood in a row before him on the cabin table. The dark-red fluid was drained to the last drop. Recorking the empty bottle, the Assyrian, forgetting that we were not out at sea, flung it through the cabin door with such force that it fell smash on the deck of a vessel astern of us, causing a gruff shout of, "Halloa! what are you at there?"

The Skipper, who was always careful of the proprieties of sea-life, stepped on deck for a moment to explain to our neighbors that the missile was un-intentionally sent in their direction.

The Assyrian, intent only on his cocktails, grasped a large stone jug which stood conveniently at hand, in a recess near the head of his berth. He elevated it in a peculiar way that he had prided himself on, which brought the body of the jug to rest in the hollow of his extended arm. At this moment the Professor, who was seated at the opposite end of the table, drew our solitary lamp toward him to light his cigar. The Assyrian, not seeing very well what he was about, decanted a pretty large allowance into each glass, and putting in a little water, handed the tumblers around and requested us to drink.

"Confusion to the fog and success to the last of the cocktails."

We drank; and then followed a general spluttering and spitting forth, accompanied by energetic requests to the Assyrian to know what on earth he had made the cocktails of?

That gentleman himself had swallowed a healthy amount, and was exhibiting alarming symptoms of strangulation. As soon as he could speak, he produced the jug and held it up for inspection. The Skipper burst into a roar of laughter.

"Why, that is the burning-fluid jug; I filled the lamp from it just before supper, and put the jug there so as to have it handy."

"Handy it was," said the Assyrian with a groan; "it has spoiled our cocktails, and for all I know, poisoned us. But what have you done with the whiskey?"

"The whiskey is all gone," replied the Skipper, "and I put the empty jug in the forepeak, where I used to keep the burning-fluid."

"Well, well," said the Assyrian, "what is swallowed, is swallowed. There is an end to cocktails. But I must have something to dilute this confounded fluid in my stomach, or I shall die of spontaneous combustion. There is a box of claret in the forepeak, Skipper; get out a couple of bottles, and let us wash down the abomination. Keep your mouth away from that lamp," he warned the Professor, who was relighting his cigar; "if your breath comes in contact with the flame, you will certainly explode, and we shall have another dreadful accident."

The Skipper produced the claret, and as the night was warm and still, we adjourned from the cabin to the deck.

It was very dark. The soft white fog enveloped us like a veil, through which we could dimly discern

113

the sea-wall of the harbor, looking, as it loomed in the haze, like some huge castle. We could see vaguely the outlines of the thronged vessels around us, and that was all. Everything was weird and mystic and ghostly in aspect. All around us were voices, but not a man was visible. We felt like those in the Arabian story who, in the enchanted forest, heard many but saw no one. Talking and laughter on every side showed that the hundreds of fishermen in the harbor were, like ourselves, on deck, enjoying the mildness of the night.

As the evening wore away we sipped our claret, smoked our cigars, and chatted over the events of the past and the projects for the future, or listened dreamily to the laughter and the talk that came so gayly out of the darkness. At length there was a momentary silence. It was broken by a song.

A rich, deep, manly voice from the Venus, a schooner that lay some distance astern of us, sang a song, full of simple, tender feeling. I cannot recall the lines, but it expressed the longing of a sailor for his home, for the scenes of his childhood, for the peace and innocence of rural life, for his mother and sisters, for the waving woods, and grassy, flowery fields. It was long, and was sung slowly and distinctly, with perfect taste and pronunciation. The most entire silence prevailed. Not a sound broke the universal hush of attention, save the low ripple of the tide pouring through the narrow entrance of the port. As the song closed there was an instant's pause, and then there resounded at once over the harbor the vehement clapping of hundreds of hard hands. It was very striking, this simultaneous and hearty applause from an invisible audience, shrouded in darkness and mist.

Presently some one on the other side of the harbor began a song which our Pilot said was called "Cape Ann." It seemed to have no meaning, or a mystical one. It began:

"We hunted and we halloed, and the first thing we did find
Was a barn in the meadow, and that we left behind.
Look ye there!"

The only allusion to Cape Ann that caught my ear was:

"We hunted and we halloed, and the next thing we did find
Was the lighthouse on Cape Ann, and that we left behind.
Look ye there!"

A good many voices joined in singing this, as if it were familarly known, but it was not applauded. The same voice began "Annie Laurie," in which also a number joined.

The voice from the Venus took up the strain of love in a song which none of us remembered to have heard or read. It was well sung, and warmly applauded. The singer continued with another song, beginning:

"When stars are in the quiet skies,
Then most I pine for thee;
Bend on me, then, thy tender eyes,
As stars look on the sea."

"Bulwer, by Jove!" exclaimed the Assyrian. "Where did the fellow pick that up, I wonder?"

"In some sailor's song-book," said the Professor. "The most popular song-books among our New England sailors abound in pieces of that sort, sentimental and poetical. You will find the best songs in the language in them. But, come, son of Semiramis, let them hear your voice. Give them something stirring, something bacchanal. With a bottle of claret down your throat, you ought to do justice to the theme."

The Assyrian, who sang finely and liked to hear his own voice, readily complied. "I'll try them with Wendell Holmes 'Song of Other Days,' though I fear it's touch above their comprehension."

"Not a bit," said the Professor, "they'll understand it as well as you do — go ahead."

And so the Assyrian lifted up his voice and sang that song which is in part so beautiful that it cannot be too often copied:

> "They say we were not born to eat;
>   But gray-haired sages think
> It means — Be moderate in your meat,
>   And partly live to drink;
> For baser tribes the rivers flow,
>   That know not wine or song;
> Man wants but little drink below.
>   But wants that little strong.
>
> ❄   ❄   ❄   ❄
>
> "Then once again, before we part,
>   My empty glass shall ring;
> And he that has the warmest heart
>   Shall loudest laugh and sing."

116

The applause was immense. Round upon round of clapping rolled over the harbor, shaking the fog and reverberating among the piles of granite.

"Do you remember, Carter," said the Assyrian, "where we heard that song before?"

"Ay, well do I remember." The question carried me back from the fogs and fishermen of Cape Ann to a far different scene in Boston, where, amid a gay circle that included some of the foremost wits and poets of New England, the brilliant Autocrat of the Breakfast Table had sung the song himself.*

"Skipper," continued the Assyrian, turning to that personage, who was sitting on the taffrail with his pipe, "take the dory and carry a bottle of claret over to the Venus, with the compliments of the Helen to the man who has been singing."

"Nonsense," said the Professor. "Don't send them claret — they will take it for bad vingear. A couple of bottles of ale will be much more acceptable."

The amendment was accepted, and in a moment or two the Skipper sculled away in the dory, his pipe gleaming through the fog like a will-o'-the-wisp. He presently returned with the thanks of the Venus for the present. The vessel, he said, was a mackerel-fisher, with eight or ten men on board, and was waiting for the fog to lift before she started for the fishing-grounds. The singer was a good-looking young man who seemed to be the mate.

The Professor, whose summer cruises in past

*Oliver Wendell Holmes.

117

years had brought him much in contact with fishermen, said they were a remarkably intelligent and
efficient body of men. A slow, stupid, lazy fellow
could not succeed in their vocation, which, as pursued on our shores, was well calculated to call out
each man's individual smartness and gumption. Of
the hundreds of fishermen then in the harbor where
we lay, probably every one had received a good
common-school education, and nine-tenths of them
were qualified, by character and intelligence, to
take command of vessels.

It was now midnight, and the air had become
chilly. So we went below and turned in to sleep.

16

CONGER EELS
FOR THE ISLES OF SHOALS

Next morning, the fog was very dense, but the sun was shining and the air soon grew hot. The old Pilot said he thought the fog would lift at noon, so we rowed the sloop out upon the ocean to be ready for the breeze if it should spring up.

Off Halibut Point the Professor dredged, but got little, the bottom being muddy. The rest of us fished, and caught, among other things, a couple of conger-eels about two feet each in length. They were yellowish white, mottled with dirty spots, the head and neck thick, the mouth large, but the body slender and snake-like. These creatures have been caught ten feet long and as thick as a man's arm. The Professor dissected those we took, and found in their stomachs a large quantity of crustaceans.

About the middle of the forenoon, to our great relief — we were heartily tired of the fog, and longed to be on our way Down East — a light southeast breeze sprung up. We started at once for the Isles of Shoals which lay nearly due north from us, about twenty miles distant. We headed somewhat easterly to counteract the current which sets into Ipswich Bay on the flood tide. The breeze increased, and we dashed on finely through the fog, keeping a sharp lookout ahead. After running about two hours, we suddenly met a large schooner bearing down on

WHITE ISLAND LIGHT

us. She emerged from the fog like a ghost, and passed close to us. Her skipper, standing on the taffrail, hailed as she swept by: "Whereaway is Cape Ann?"

"Ten or twelve miles south by west," responded our Pilot, who said the stranger was a mackerel vessel, probably on her way home from the Isles of Shoals. In a moment she vanished into the mist.

Soon after this the fog began to clear away, which it did rapidly and beautifully, curling and wreathing and rolling off its soft fleeces whiter than wool, until they melted into thin air. Then, far off before us, we saw on the horizon a white spot, like an immense ship, or like a house built right in the sea. This, the Pilot said, was White Island Lighthouse, the southernmost point of the Isles of Shoals.

At 2:30 the blue peak of Agamenticus, a mountain on the coast of Maine, appeared in sight beyond the Isles. It is seen to a vast distance on the ocean, and is a noted landmark among the fishermen and seamen who navigate these stormy waters. About 4 o'clock we reached the islands, running through a squadron of seine-boats, cruising for mackerel, and passing close to a high conical rock, rising like a haystack from the water, on the top of which stood a picturesque group of red-shirted fishermen watching for mackerel schools.

We ran to the westward of the southern islands for some distance, and then hauled up and entered the harbor, which is a sort of roadstead, where we anchored between Star Island and Appledore, famous in song and story.

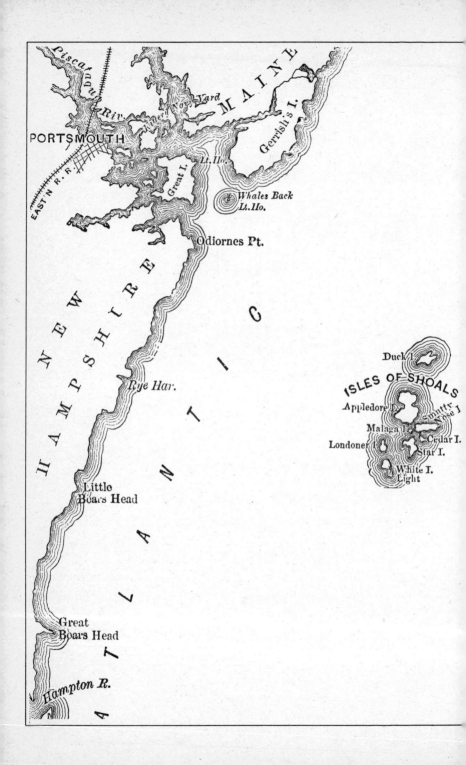

17

THE ISLES OF SHOALS
THE PRINCE OF APPLEDORE
NIGHT ON THE WATER

The Isles of Shoals form a group of eight small rocky islets, lying close together, about nine miles from the Portsmouth lighthouses. The largest of them, Appledore, has an area of three hundred and fifty acres, or a little more than half a square mile. Star Island, the next in size, comprises one hundred and fifty acres; Haley's, the third in extent, about one hundred.* The five other isles are mere rocks, the largest measuring not more than eight acres in extent.

These islands were discovered in 1614 by Captain John Smith, the founder of Virginia, and seem at one time to have been of some importance. It is on record, I believe, that a session of the Provincial Legislature of New Hampshire was once held here; and on Appledore there was once a courthouse and a church, though now the only buildings on the island are a summer hotel and one or two deserted houses. For a century before the Revolution the population of the group had risen to six hundred.

---

*Haley's is now called Smuttynose.

Now it numbers only a hundred, who live chiefly in a village on Star Island, off which our vessel lay. William Pepperell, an ancestor of Sir William Pepperell, the taker of Louisburg, was among the first settlers at the Shoals, and there, in the fisheries, became rich and laid the foundation of the fortunes of his family.

STAR ISLAND MEETING-HOUSE

The neighborhood of the Isles is a famous fishing-ground, and as soon as we had cast anchor we got out our lines. The water was very deep, and we caught plenty of pollack weighing two or three pounds apiece, cunners a foot in length, and several cod and haddock. After fishing awhile, the Professor determined to try his luck with the dredge in the harbor. The Artist and I got the Pilot to row us in the dory to Appledore, whose huge five-storied hotel, perched on the western side, excited our curiosity. We landed with difficulty on the steep and slippery rocks, and the Pilot returned to the sloop to take the Professor and his dredge.

The Artist and I rambled for an hour or two over Appledore, which is nothing but a huge rock, nearly a mile in length, with an elevation at the highest of sixty feet above the sea. It is seamed with fissures,

APPLEDORE ISLAND

apparently the work of earthquakes, for no other power is adequate to their production. The vegetation is of the scantiest — a little grass, a few bushes, an elm and a cherry tree, and a patch of potatoes a few rods square, was all that we could discover. A small green snake was the only wild animal I saw. The tame ones were a cow and a few sheep.

We found the landlord of the hotel, the proprietor and prince of the island, sitting on the broad veranda watching the western sky. He was immensely stout and jolly. He told us he had not been off the island for thirteen years, and pretended to be much surprised at our fondness for wandering about, when we might stay quietly at home. Our projected visit to Grand Manan, he spoke of as one would a voyage to the Antarctic. In early life he had been a member of the New Hampshire Legislature and an active politician, but a disappointment of some kind, perhaps of love, perhaps of ambitions, had led him to obtain the office of keeper of White Island Light, on which lonely, storm-beaten rock he had passed many years, cut off from mankind more completely than any hermit. Tired at length of his isolation, he had relinquished his office and settled on Apple-dore, which, though more extensive in territory, was hardly more populous than his lighthouse rock, except for a few months in summer.

Returning to the shore of the island, we saw far off the Professor, in his red shirt, busily dredging, with the Pilot rowing the dory. We had, of course, to wait their pleasure to be taken off. So, after exploring a ruined house near by, we seated ourselves on the rocks and watched the purple sunset behind the blue mountains on the mainland. In the course of half an hour the Professor returned to the sloop with the spoils of his dredging, and, after putting him on board, the Pilot came back and took us off the rocks — not without difficulty, so steep and slippery with seaweed was the shore.

Among other things, the Professor had drawn up from the bottom some specimens of the northern spider-crab. This creature is very sluggish, and consequently becomes so overgrown with seaweeds and polyps as to resemble a walking forest rather than a crab. Its covering serves for concealment, and two glistening eyes among the foliage, forever on the watch for prey, enable him to spy and seize many an unlucky mollusk who creeps unsuspectingly near.

Night came, and with it a slight mist which glorified while it partially veiled the surrounding objects. There were several mackerel-jiggers in the harbor from Swampscott and Cape Ann, and their officers visited us to inquire for news. As we sat on deck chatting and smoking, I was struck with the wildly picturesque nature of the scene. The moon was up, and her light, blending and struggling with the soft, drifting mist, disclosed glimpses of the rocky ribs against which the low rote of the sea was sounding. Southward, at no great distance, White Island light was revolving, heightening, as it now appeared and now disappeared, the weird impression of the moonlight and the mist. Presently a large schooner came gliding into the harbor, coming out of the mist with a silent, ghost-like suddenness, the effect of which upon the imagination is unlike any phenomenon of the land that I have ever witnessed.

18

THE E PLURIBUS UNUM
THE MONKFISH
TO PORTSMOUTH AND PORTLAND

Next morning we all went, after breakfast, to visit a Swampscott mackerel schooner, the E Pluribus Unum, which lay at anchor not far off. On our way to her, we saw horse-mackerel swimming about the harbor with their sharp fins sticking out of the water. This huge fish is the tunny of the Mediterranean, where it swims in large schools, and is caught in great quantities, especially off the coast of Sicily. They are comparatively rare on our coast, and these were the first we had seen, though we heard of them almost every day. They are found sometimes fifteen feet in length, and weighing a thousand pounds. Their flesh is good eating, looking like young pork, and tasting like the finest mackerel. The men of the island caught them with harpoons.

The E Pluribus Unum was a fine, clean vessel of thirty-six tons. We went on board partly to see the vessel, partly to grind bait, and partly to see a "bait-mill," which to the Assyrian, the Artist, and myself was an entirely novel institution. In fishing for mackerel with line and hook from the side of a vessel, the first thing done is to throw over bait to attract the fish to the surface. This bait consists of hardheads or other poor fish cut up into very small pieces, generally by being ground in a mill. The bait-mill consists of an oblong wooden box, standing on one end, and containing a roller armed with knives, which is turned by a crank on the outside. It cuts up the bait very expeditiously.

From the E Pluribus Unum we went ashore to look at the curiosities of the isles, which are all of a melancholy and sinister nature. The first and most famous is a chasm in the rocks called Betty Moody's Cave. Early in colonial times the Indians from the mainland made a descent upon the islands, and killed or carried off all the inhabitants except a Mrs. Moody, who hid herself under the rocks with her two small children. The Indians made sharp search for fugitives, and the unhappy mother, unable to keep her infants quiet, killed them with a knife to prevent their crying from attracting the attention of the savages to her hiding-place.

Another spot among the rocks on the shore was the favorite resort of Miss Underhill, a young lady from New Hampshire who taught school at the island for two or three years. She was sitting there reading on the 11th of September, 1848, when a huge wave came and swept her off into the ocean, never to be seen again on earth. Another place of tragic interest is marked by the graves of sixteen shipwrecked mariners washed ashore in a storm. They lie side by side, each with a stone at his head and feet.

From some fishermen on shore we got a monkfish which they had just taken in a seine. This hideous monster is known among the fishermen by many names. It is called "widegab" because its mouth is so large sometimes that a man's head might be put in it. The term "angler" is derived from its habits. It lies on the bottom, concealed in mud and weeds, with two or three hair-like filaments sticking up from its head, looking not unlike certain marine worms of which other fishes are fond, who, seeing these apparent worms, approach to eat them, and are seized by the lurking "angler," who is too sluggish to catch his prey by active pursuit.

The specimen we got measured forty-four inches in length and thirty inches in breadth. It weighed thirty pounds. We took it on board, disembowelled it, filled it with salt, sewed it up and packed it with salt in a box, which we directed to the Smithsonian Institute at Washington and forwarded the same day by express from Portsmouth.

The morning had been foggy; but at 11 a.m. the mist rose, and we raised anchor and made sail for Portsmouth. Outside the harbor we passed a number of seine-boats watching for mackerel. These boats are each manned by six men, and are accompanied by three smaller boats with one man in each, which row around and keep the mackerel in a body while the seine is being cast. After the seine is thrown, its edges are drawn into the large boat, leaving the mackerel in the center of the seine, from which they are scooped out into the small boats and carried ashore.

We had a fine southerly breeze, and in somewhat more than an hour had passed the Whale's Back Lighthouse, romantically situated on a rock in the sea, and had come to anchor inside of Fort Constitution, off New Castle, a village three miles

WHALE'S BACK LIGHTHOUSE

below Portsmouth at the mouth of the Piscataqua. The tide soon turning, and running very strongly up the river, we took advantage of it, and ran up to Portsmouth, where we fastened the sloop to a wharf, and went ashore to get our letters and make some purchases.

The city — a quiet, clean, aristocratic-looking place of ten or twelve thousand inhabitants — is beautifully situated on a peninsula on the south side of the river, the land sloping gently toward the water. The harbor is remarkably commodious, well protected from every wind, and with forty feet of water at low tide. The river opposite the city seemed to be nearly a mile wide, with a very rapid current, moving at least five miles an hour.

PORTSMOUTH

At 6 p.m. we dropped down to our former anchorage at New Castle. On our way down we were greatly pleased with the sight of the workmen at the Navy Yard — which is on an island opposite Portsmouth — crossing the river in boats, returning to their homes in the city after the conclusion of the day's labor. It was the largest flotilla of boats I ever saw, and was a very gay and animated scene.

While the Pilot was getting supper ready, the rest of us went ashore to visit the fort, which was built in 1808 on the site, I believe, of an old British fort. We were very civilly received by the keeper, Sargeant Davison, who, with his wife and children constitute the entire garrison at present. We found him an intelligent and communicative man, and remarkably young-looking for a soldier who had been in the service forty-one years. The fort mounts forty-six guns, mostly twenty-four pounders. The ramparts command a beautiful view of land and ocean, and we lingered upon them till long after sunset, watching the passing ships, and the lighthouses flaring up as the sun went down, and listening to the talk of the old soldier about his battles and adventures. He had fought through the Mexican war, and had served for many years in Florida against the Indians.

Soon after supper we were boarded by one of the pilots of the harbor, who was so drunk that he became disagreeable, and we had to suggest pretty clearly that he take his departure, which he accordingly did. If his condition was typical, it is a proof of the excellence of Portsmouth harbor that vessels get in at all under such guidance.

The next morning (Sunday, July 18) was clear and mild, with a fair and gentle breeze from the south. We got under way at 7 o'clock, and, passing out of the harbor, steered to the northeast, keeping about two miles from the shore. We were soon surrounded by large schools of mackerel, and as we wanted some for dinner, we laid to and tried to "toll" them, as the fishermen call it, by throwing over handfulls of our minced bait. But we could not get a bite. The Professor took the dory and rowed repeatedly into the middle of a school with no better success. The fish would not touch the bait.

The weather was delightful, and we basked luxuriously on deck, gazing at the picturesque coast, with its hills, headlands, and towns sparkling in the sun, or watching the rippling mackerel as they cruised about us, or occasionally dipping up a sunsquall, of which vast numbers were floating by. Toward noon we reached Cape Neddick, or rather, Cape Neddick's Nubble, a huge and high rocky promontory which juts far out into the sea, and is visible from a great distance. We sailed close by to enable the Artist to make a sketch of it.

About an hour after we passed Cape Neddick, a sudden storm of wind and rain rose up right ahead of us, presenting a very singular appearance. We were sailing in the most brilliant sunshine, and straight before us to the north, at the distance of a mile, the air was filled with a dense, black, scowling cloud, which came driving down upon us with fearful velocity. We lowered our mainsail, and the squall swept by, deluging us with rain, and causing the little sloop to shiver and reel with the blow. We were, happily, not in the mid-path of the whirlwind; but I suppose touched only an edge of it. Its direction was toward the southwest, and it broke with fury on the mainland. On the sea, the sky soon cleared up, and we kept on our northeast course.

At 6 p.m. we were near Cape Elizabeth, and had a fine view of the White Mountains of New Hampshire, Mount Washington bearing northwest by north. At sunset, off Cape Elizabeth, it fell calm, and we lay and watched the lighthouses and the moon. The two lights looked like large stars near the horizon, and formed the corners of a triangle of which the moon was the apex.

About 8 p.m. a breeze sprang up from the northwest, and we began to beat up into Portland harbor through a large fleet of coasters bound southward, which were taking advantage of the wind to come out to sea. The tide as well as the wind was against us, and it was not till 3 o'clock the next morning that we reached a safe anchorage, between House and Peake's Islands. We were still several miles from the city, and were glad enough to turn in and get some sleep.

At daybreak the seamen got the sloop under way without disturbing us, and, on awaking about breakfast time, we found the Helen moored alongside a wharf at Portland. Discarding our sea-stained shirts and trousers, we donned our best attire, and went ashore, to spend a day or two with our friends in the city.

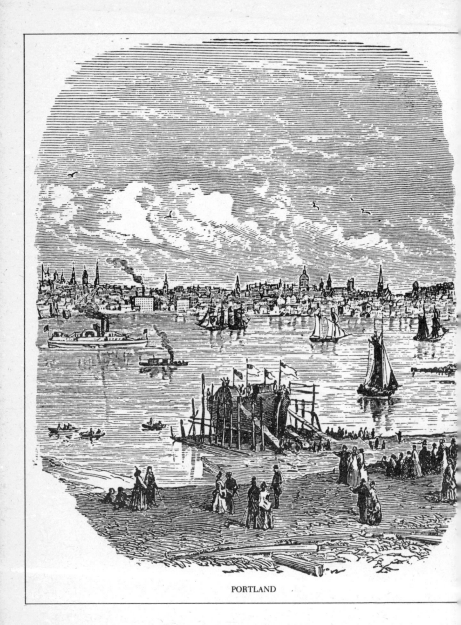

PORTLAND

19

CASCO BAY
THE POWER OF MELODY
THE HADDOCK
JEWELL'S ISLAND*

No July morning was ever finer than that on which we bade adieu to Portland, and turned our little sloop toward the nearest of the countless isles of Casco Bay. As the gentle breeze swept the Helen slowly over the sparkling waters, we spread on the top of the cabin the charts of the coast of Maine with which our good friends in Portland had provided us, and fell to diligent study of our proposed route.

Casco Bay extends from Cape Elizabeth on the west, to Cape Small Point on the east, a distance of about twenty miles. It is an indentation in the coast whose greatest depth does not exceed fifteen miles. Beside Portland, at its western end, there are three or four flourishing towns on the shores of the bay; and embosomed in its waters, if the popular account be true, are no less than three hundred and sixty-five islands, a compliment to the days of the year which is also attributed to Lake George, Lake Winnipesaukee, and several other bodies of water. Without vouching for the exact number, it is doubtless safe to say that there are at least three hundred isles and islets, beside many bold and picturesque headlands and peninsulas, so that scarcely anywhere else in the world can you find a more varied or more lovely commingling of land and water.

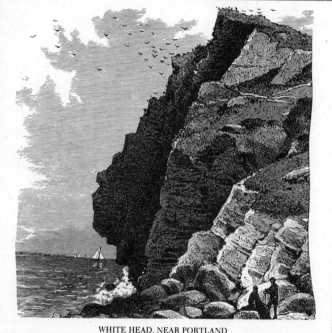

WHITE HEAD, NEAR PORTLAND

The shores of the islands and the promontories are mostly covered with woods of maple, oak, beech, pine, and fir, growing nearly to the water's edge, and throwing their shadows over many a deep inlet and winding channel. It is impossible to conceive of any combination of scenery more charming, more romantic, more captivating to the eye, or more sug-

138

gestive to the imagination. No element of beauty is wanting. Many of the islands are wildly picturesque in form, and from their woodland summits you behold on the one hand the surges of the Atlantic, breaking almost at your feet, and on the other the placid waters of the bay, spangled by gems of emerald, while in the distance you discern the peaks of the White Mountains.

For several hours we sauntered, rather than sailed, through this enchanted and enchanting fairyland, steering hither and thither as caprice impelled, or as the perpetually-changing views attracted. At length the Skipper, whose taste for the picturesque was yet undeveloped, and who beside was sufficiently familiar with beauties of the bay, began to hint that it was time to think of dinner, and that a few fresh fish would lend additional grace to that ceremony. We anchored in deep water, in a broad channel called Hussey's Sound. The Pilot kindled his fire in the furnace at the companion-way, and we baited our lines and began to fish.

For more than an hour we fished without a bite. We suggested to the Skipper that our lines were not cast in pleasant places, and that we had better shift our ground. But that worthy, who had an innate repugnance to hoisting the mainsail oftener than he was obliged to, held for some moments silent and mysterious communion with the sky, the water, and the neighboring shores, and then confidently predicted that the fish would soon bite. Having considerable faith in his penetration into the whims and ways of our finny friends, and suspecting that in this instance his judgment was based upon observation of the state of the tide, we patiently pursued our sport, if sport it could be called.

The Assyrian, who was prone to easy postures, had been for the last half-hour lying on his back with his hands clasped on the top of his head, and his feet, about which he had fastened his line, protruding over the low rail of the sloop. He now began to sing a song, which began:

"The grasshopper sat on the sweet-potato vine,
  Up came the turkey-gobbler and yanked him off behind."

The second stanza, intended to show the careless security of the grasshopper, was next sung:

"The grasshopper sat on the sweet-potato vine,
  Up came the turkey-gobbler and yanked him off behind."

Then followed the third stanza, illustrating the trickery of the turkey-gobbler:

"The grasshopper sat on the sweet-potato vine,
  Up came the turkey-gobbler and yanked him off behind."

This elegant ditty was interrupted by a bite which nearly "yanked" the minstrel into the water. He rolled over and scrambled to his feet with remarkable agility, exclaiming, as he hauled in his line, "A halibut at last, I think!" To catch a halibut had been for some time the main object of the Assyrian's ambition, and the farther east we went the more confident he became that every large fish he hooked would prove to be the prize. I observed, however that the old Pilot, who always grew excited at the prospect of halibut, after one eager glance at the line, turned with indifference to his furnace, on which he had a large iron pot bubbling with water, all ready for a cod or haddock, or even for a pollack if nothing better could be got. There was evidently no hope of halibut yet.

The capture proved to be a skate — a flat, broad, brown-backed monster, with a dirty-white belly, a tail like a monkey's, and a spade-shaped snout with powerful teeth. He was very large — about three feet in length — and it required a good deal of careful management to get him aboard without breaking the cod-line. The creature was very angry, and furiously lashed the deck with its tail, squeaking and writhing in a droll manner.

The capture of the skate did not materially improve our prospect of dinner, for though the Professor proposed to cook the creature, the Pilot would not hear of such an abomination. In vain he was assured that it was a favorite fish in the markets of London, Paris, and Edinburgh; in vain I cited to him the Rev. Badham's assertion that all skate is eatable, though not all equally good; in vain the Professor assured him that Galen, in his treatise on ailments, particularly recommends the flesh of the skate as agreeable in flavor and light of digestion. His objections were immovable. At length the Assyrian, who had a bad habit of inventing quotations, recited to him an imaginary passage of Aristotle about the obstinacy of fishermen with regard to the edible qualities of the skate.

"Damn Aristotle!" responded the old fisherman; "don't you suppose I know what fish are fit to eat?" With the aid of the Skipper, he tossed the monster overboard, and seizing a line, he said he would soon give us something worth cooking. Sure enough, in a few minutes, he pulled up a haddock weighing about seven pounds — as we judged by the eye, for we were too anxious for dinner to delay his transfer to the pot by putting him to the test of the steelyards.

As cooked by the Pilot, we pronounced the haddock excellent; and after dinner we raised the anchor, hoisted sail, and cruised idly among the islands till near sunset, when we put into a delicious little cove — narrow, deep, and shady — on Jewell's Island. As we glided in, an old fisherman who resided on the island came alongside in his dory to have a little chat, and gave us a magnificent lobster, which went immediately into the pot for supper. After coming to anchor, we all went ashore in our boat, except the Pilot, who was detained on board by his duties as cook, to explore the island, witness the sunset, and get milk, eggs, and butter from a farm-house near our landing-place.

The island, which lies about ten miles east of Portland, seemed to be fertile and well cultivated. The farmhouse was built on elevated ground, and the view of the sunset and of the island-studded bay was superb. Fresh and sweet were the eggs and milk and butter with which we returned to our sloop, and very jolly the supper we had in the little cabin. The evening was pleasantly cool, and the Assyrian, remarking that boiled lobster was not wholesome unless well qualified with something acid, availed himself of the Pilot's steaming teakettle and brewed a pitcher of hot lemonade with a strong infusion of whiskey, which he administered to each of us in proper doses, as a sure preventive against any ill effects from our supper.

20

The next morning, Wednesday, was fair and warm. We rose early, and, after breakfasting on rock-cod and blue-perch which the Artist caught alongside, we resumed our cruise among the islands. We skirted the shores of one of the largest of these, Great Chebeague, and landed on its neighbor, Chebeague, around which we walked, picking up shells on its beaches and exploring caverns in its rocks. Toward noon the wind freshened, blowing fair and strong for Harpswell Point. We stretched across a broad expanse of the bay for that place, which the Skipper, who had formerly resided there, said was more beautiful than anything we had yet seen. We were running along pretty rapidly when the Skipper, who had the helm, began to show symptoms of uneasiness. It was so many years, he said, since he had sailed these waters, that he was not quite sure of his course — there were a good many sunken reefs in this part of the bay.

The Professor brought out the Coast Survey chart, and he and I attempted to spread it on the top of the cabin, but the wind was blowing too hard for that. We carried it below and spread it on the cabin table. We had just begun to examine it when my attention was arrested by a strange grinding and pounding sound apparently just beneath my feet, under the cabin floor. I had never heard anything like it, and had not the least suspicion of its cause. I glanced at the Professor, who turned pale and darted on deck. He had heard that sound once before, while cruising on the coast of Japan, and under circumstances not likely to make him forgetful of its meaning.

I followed him to the deck. The Skipper stood with the helm in his hand, looking sheepish. The Assyrian and the Artist were staring wildly about them, while the prompt old Pilot, though suddenly roused from a nap he had been taking on the shady side of the deck, had already let go the jib and was lowering the mainsail. Our vessel had run her length onto a reef, and was stuck fast about a mile from land. Fortunately the tide was rising, and in the course of an hour, by carrying out an anchor astern and hauling with all our strength, we succeeded in getting her off without any great damage. Stationing the Assyrian and the Artist at the bow, with instructions to keep a sharp lookout for rocks, we ran a few miles farther, and, entering the heart-shaped bay at the end of Harpswell Point, anchored in deep water, not far from its eastern shore.

As the Skipper said that this was a good place for fish, we got out our lines while the Pilot was getting dinner. Before we had caught anything the meal was ready, and we went below, leaving our lines in the water in hopes of finding that some fish had been foolish enough to hook himself during our absence.

It so happened that I was first on deck after dinner. I tried the lines, but found nothing caught. The Assyrian's line was over the stern, and, as the tide was running very fast, he had let it out to its whole length of several hundred feet. I hauled it in to see that it was still baited, and as no one had yet followed me out of the cabin, I took the opportunity to play the Assyrian a trick. A huge stone jug weighing many pounds, and capable of holding several gallons, stood near me on the deck empty. It was our principal water jug, and the Skipper had placed it there to have it handy, intending to take it ashore and fill it after he had cleared away the dinner things. The temptation was irresistible. I tied the end of my friend's line to the handle of the jug, and lowered it overboard. The tide swept it far along until it had gurgled full of water, when of course it sank plumb. I returned to my own line, and presently caught a large cod, the sound of whose flapping on deck brought out my comrades.

The Assyrian, cigar in mouth, sat down on the taffrail and gently fingered his line, with the air of a man who has had a satisfactory dinner and does not yet care to exert himself to catch fish for supper. Presently, however, he had a bite, and began languidly to pull up his line. The unusual weight soon made itself felt. The Assyrian grew suddenly excited. He said nothing about halibut, for previous disappointments had made him cautious on that point, but halibut was in his mind by the way he handled his line, holding it in readiness to yield in case the monster should suddenly put forth his strength. We gathered round to witness the struggle. The Assyrian tugged and tugged, growing gradually more and more astonished at the weight of his capture and the passive nature of its resistance, for the halibut, as the fisherman often told us, never yields without a desperate and powerful contest. At length his prize reached the surface. Without remark the Assyrian quietly lifted it on board, amid roars of laughter, and as he passed into the cabin to relight his cigar, good-humoredly nodded to me, saying:

"I'll pay you for that, my boy, before you are much older." He kept his word.

By and by the Skipper put the jug into the boat, and the Assyrian and I went ashore with him to a fisherman's cottage, the only house in sight. I had been struck, as I saw it from the deck of the sloop, with the singular beauty of the place.

The men of the fisherman's family were away, but there were several women at the house, who received us kindly and gave us milk and berries. The Assyrian speedily made himself at home with the ladies, and when I proposed to go to the beach, about two hundred yards from the house, to take an ocean bath, he refused to accompany me, but offered to wait where he was till I came back. The Skipper had gone to his sloop with his jug of water, to invite the Artist and Professor on shore to partake also of milk and berries. So I went alone to the sea, and strolled along the beach till I came to a convenient pile of rocks, out of sight of the house, and took off my clothes, and went in.

The water was awfully cold, and being unable to swim, and so not daring to plunge boldly, I endured fearful torture in the effort to get a thorough bath. A few rods farther along from where I went in, there was a large rock almost covered by the water, to which I decided to go, calculating that by the time I could reach it and return, I should have had as much sea-bathing as it was desirable or possible to endure.

I reached it easily enough, and after clinging to it for a moment thoroughly chilled, turned to go to the shore.

Imagine my dismay at beholding, as I looked around, a woman approaching along the beach from the direction of the house. A tall, elderly female, wearing a veil and carrying a parasol. Evidently she was bent on a seaside stroll. She would have seen me if she had looked in my direction, for the distance that separated us was inconsiderable. But she walked with her eyes cast down, either wrapped in thought or searching for shells and pebbles, I could not determine which. Nor did it much matter. I was nearly dead with cold, but of course could not quit the shelter of the water while the lady was in sight. If she only kept onward, however slowly, I thought I could hold out, for thank Heaven! there was a rocky point at no great distance which would conceal me from view as soon as she should pass it. So

I crouched behind the rock to which I was clinging, shuddering with anguish as the chill waves rolled in succession over me.

The lady was provokingly slow. She lingered, she stopped, she stooped to examine every shell and every pebble. I grew almost frantic with suffering, and was twenty times on the point of crying out, and warning her off. Still, I trusted she would pass without seeing me, and thought I could endure a little longer.

At length she reached the rocks, among which I had deposited my clothes. She did not notice the garments apparently, but, after pausing for a minute, coolly sat down, and, to my horror and despair, pulled a book from under her shawl and began to read.

I could stand it no longer. All the tales I had ever heard of persons who had died from staying too long in the water rushed upon my memory. I felt convinced that I was not only blue around the mouth, but blue all over. It seemed as if I had been in the water at least two hours. I should certainly die. But death itself was preferable to this infernal cold, which caused my very bones to ache. Positively I could stand it no longer.

I began by coughing, gently at first, afterward more vigorously. It did no good. She was absorbed in her book, some foolish novel, doubtless — confound the author! I hemmed, hawed, hooted.

I splashed the water. All to no effect. A horrible thought flashed across me: perhaps she was deaf. I tried to get a stone from the bottom to throw at her, or rather near her, in hopes of attracting her attention, but found I could not reach bottom without putting my head under water. It suddenly occurred to me that the tide was rising, and that my post would no longer be tenable even if I could stand the cold. That settled the question.

"Hallo! hallo there!" I shouted with all the force of my lungs.

"Hallo, yourself! What are you making such a row for? Aren't you ashamed to yell at a lady in that way?"

I recognized the voice at the first word, and was beside the speaker before the sentence was finished. Throwing up the veil, which had concealed his features, the Assyrian burst into a laugh, in which, though at first I thought of stoning him, I finally joined. He had persuaded the women at the cottage to lend him his disguise, in order to repay me, as he had promised, for the affair of the jug.

A smart run on the beach in the warm air relieved me of the chill I had got in the water. Being soon after joined by the Professor and the Artist, we rambled till sunset amid the groves and glades and rocks and beaches of the peninsula, which we all agreed far surpassed Nahant in beauty, while it almost exactly resembled it in situation. The sunset, as we watched it from a lofty bank crowned with trees, was glorious. Our view extended over Casco Bay to the mainland beyond, and farther still to the White Mountains, of which we had never from any point obtained a more beautiful or more impressive view.

We lingered long after Mount Washington had vanished in the gloom of twilight, and then, descending to the shore, assented fully to the patriotic remark of the Skipper, as he rowed us to the sloop, that "There wasn't a finer place in the world than Harpswell."

21

SUCCESSFUL FISHING
WHITING, HAKE, AND COD
A CHOWDER-PARTY

The next morning, when I came out of the little cabin of the sloop, the sky was gray with the faint light of dawn, and a few of the largest stars were yet visible. The air was fresh and fragrant, and the water of the bay looked singularly cool and clear, as it swayed and eddied with the rushing of the tide. The distant isles seemed shadowy and spectral in the morning mist, and from the groves on the Point came the twitter of land-birds, occasionally breaking into song; while overhead a couple of large sea-birds were slowly wheeling in eccentric orbit, as they scanned the depths in search of prey.

Presently the old Pilot came on deck, and, as he filled and lighted his pipe, he scrutinized the sky, and said we should have a hot day. He then began his preparations for breakfast, and, after calling my comrades to come on deck and see the sun rise, I fished from the side of our vessel, and soon caught flounders and cod sufficient for our morning meal. After breakfast, we went ashore for a farewell look at Harpswell Point and its romantic groves of pine and cedar, and its stately oaks and maples. On returning to the sloop, we made sail, and were soon gliding slowly onward with a gentle breeze that scarcely ruffled the water. At the end of an hour, the breeze, faint as it was, grew fainter still, and we came to anchor in a channel, where we had in every direction charming views through long and liquid vistas edged with green islands. It was also, the Skipper said, a famous place for fish.

We got out our lines and had good luck, catching cod and haddock in abundance, and also, in lesser quantity, whiting and hake. The whiting were small, none of them more than a foot in length. They were the genuine whiting, a handsome fish, elegantly formed, the head and upper part of the body of a lead color, and the sides and belly white. When perfectly fresh it is very sweet and palatable, but its softness will not admit of its being kept long. It prefers a sandy bottom, and generally swims in schools a few miles from the shore.

The hake is much larger than the whiting, and varies in size from three pounds to thirty. One of those that we captured weighed twelve pounds, and was upward of three feet in length. The upper part of the fish is of a grayish brown; the lower part is somewhat lighter. They are caught with the hook on muddy bottoms, and bite best at night. Sometimes a single fisherman, after spending the night in "haking," as they call it, will come home in the morning with a boat-load exceeding a ton in weight.

The cod is so well known that any description of it will seem superfluous, and yet there must be millions of persons in the United States to whom the fish is an utter stranger, except in its dried and salted condition. For such readers, I will say that it has a long, smooth, and well-shaped body; the back is of a light olive-green color, with numerous reddish or yellowish spots; the belly is dusky white. The general run of cod are about two feet in length, and weigh three or four pounds, though the fish sometimes grows to great size. Immense quantities are caught on the coasts of Norway and Greenland, but the great cod-fishing ground of the world is the banks of Newfoundland. They seek their food near the bottom, and are therefore always taken with lines, and not with nets. They will bite at almost any bait, but our fishermen generally tempt them with clams.

The cod-fishery of the United States employs two thousand vessels, and about ten thousand men, and is carried on almost exclusively from New England. The vessels generally used are schooners of about eighty tons burden. About thirty millions of fish are annually taken, and their value, when dried and salted, is $2,000,000. The French cod-fishery at Newfoundland is as productive as the American, and employs about as many men, but the vessels used are generally three times as large, and consequently fewer in number.

Our fishing was at length interrupted by a circumstance in itself indicative of success: we had used up all our bait. The Pilot, seizing a spade and bucket, jumped into the dory, into which I followed him, and rowed to the nearest island. We walked across a cornfield to the other side, where a broad, muddy shore spread its blackness before us. There were no traces to my eyes of clams — and, in fact, nothing was visible but black mud, mixed with sand enough to make it sufficiently firm to bear our footsteps. But the Pilot at a glance selected a spot where, on digging, we disclosed a bed of happy mollusks — "Happy as a clam" being a proverb on the coast.

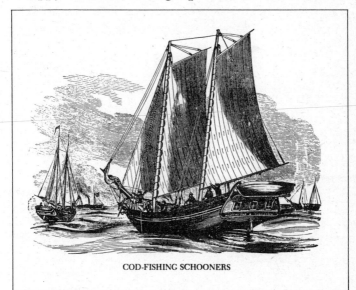

COD-FISHING SCHOONERS

While he was filling the bucket I climbed over a huge rock that bounded on one side the cove of the clams, and found beyond it a beautiful gravel beach, where I was soon busily engaged in picking up shells of a brilliant yellow color. By the time I had filled my hat with these, the Pilot had obtained sufficient bait, and we returned to the sloop, where the fishing was resumed with such luck that by dinner time we had captured more than a hundred fish of a large size.

We now thought it time to stop. The Pilot overhauled our pile, and as he handled each fish in its turn, he put some aside on the deck for preservation, and others he threw overboard. Notwithstanding this sifting out, enough remained to more than supply our wants for several days. The Skipper said that after dinner he would salt them in case we caught nothing on the morrow.

A brilliant idea suddenly struck the Assyrian as he was wiping his face after washing it, on the top of the cabin.

"I say," he exclaimed, looking round with a countenance glowing partly with the rubbing he had given it, and partly with delight at the new idea, "let us have a chowder."

It was an inspiration. "A chowder," we echoed; "why didn't we think of it before?"

"Captain," said the Professor to the Pilot, "can you make a chowder?"

The old man had just lighted the chips in his furnace, and was down on his knees blowing them into a flame. He looked up, with a strong degree of scorn on his honest face.

"Can I make a chowder?" he repeated. "Well, I should think I could; I've made more'n forty thousand."

The Professor remarked that that large figure must be only a figure of speech, for to make forty thousand chowders in sixty years would require an average of two a day.

"Well, well," said the old man, "I didn't mean forty thousand exactly. I never kept count on 'em; but I've made a great many — and if you like, I'll give you as good a one as Daniel Webster himself ever turned out."

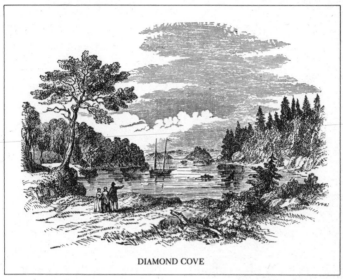

DIAMOND COVE

He went to work, and as we had salt pork, potatoes, and onions on board, and plenty of "hard tack," or crackers, in less than an hour we were sitting in front of as fine a chowder as one could wish to eat. Our morning sport had given us good appetites, and the chowder rapidly vanished, much to the delight of the Pilot, who was not a little proud of his culinary skill. We had lighted our cigars, and the Assyrian was brewing a mighty pitcher of what he persisted in calling lemonade, especially since

157

we had got within the bounds of the State of Maine, when suddenly we heard a shout.

"Sloop ahoy!" We went on deck. A yacht, crowded with ladies and gentlemen, was lying within hailing distance. "Have you got any fish?"

"Plenty. Do you want some?"

They answered with a joyful shout, and four of the gentlemen were soon on board. One of them proved to be an acquaintance of ours from Portland. They had set out on an excursion to Diamond Cove, and had been fishing all the morning, with scant luck. We gave them fish enough, and the Assyrian invited them into the cabin to partake of his favorite liquor, which he was fond of recommending as a wholesome beverage nowhere condemned in Scripture, and not contraband to Maine law, so long as you called it lemonade. He gravely corrected one of the strangers who spoke of it as punch.

Learning that the yacht had nothing to drink on board but ale, the Assyrian insisted on sending to them a pailful of his lemonade, with the compliments of the Helen. The Skipper in our dory accordingly accompanied the strangers back to their vessel, bearing with him the steaming oblation, together with a dozen of our best fish. They received the present with a cheer, and making sail for Diamond Cove, were soon out of sight among the islands.

22

Shortly after their departure we got under way, and as the sloop began to move, the Professor threw over the dredge. In a few minutes it was full, and we hauled it up, and found among the contents several rare shells, fine specimens of starfishes, and, what was then new to me, a number of sea-onions and sea-cucumbers. These last are living creatures. The sea-onion resembles a large vegetable onion, cut in two longitudinally; and the sea-cucumber, in size, shape, and color, is so similar to its namesake of the land that we were almost tempted to slice it up and try it with vinegar. The length of the sea-cucumber is from four to eight inches, but it possesses the power of extending or contracting its body at will. Its head, when the animal is alarmed, is so concealed as to be almost imperceptible, but, if it be placed in a bucket of sea-water, and left awhile undisturbed, the head will be gradually protruded and expanded, until it assumes the appearance of a beautiful flower, generally of a brilliant rose-color.

As the Pilot and Skipper wished for news from home, we directed our course to Herring Gut, an anchorage between Bailey's Island and Jaquiss, which is much frequented by fishermen, and we could hardly fail to find there some vessel fresh from Swampscott. We anchored about the middle of the afternoon, among a small fleet of schooners, with whose crews our seamen were soon in deep conference about persons and affairs on the North Shore of Massachusetts Bay.

Leaving them to enjoy their gossip on board of a Swampscott schooner, we rowed the dory into a charming little nook on the rocky shore of Jaquiss, and landed to explore the island. It proved to be a perfect gem of the sea. Like many of these islands of Casco Bay, it has long been used as a pasture for sheep, and to protect the flocks from the wind a thick belt of the original forest of evergreens has been left growing all around the shore. These trees, kept sacred from the axe and permitted to grow at their own sweet will, bent only by the storms of ocean, are as wildly picturesque as poet or artist could desire. The sheltered interior was a meadow, interspersed with copses and clumps of oaks and maples, some of them of great size. No house or barn, or sign of human occupancy, broke the solitude of the island, which was not marred even by a fence, the encircling sea confining the sheep more securely than a wall. A pond in the centre, fed by springs and garlanded by lilies, gave the animals drink.

From the summit of the island the view was superb, embracing on one side the ocean dotted with sails, and on the other, across the little roadstead where our vessel lay amid its kindred craft, the pleasant groves and fertile fields of Bailey's Island, and beyond, the far-stretching peninsulas of Harpswell and the countless isles of the bay.

The Professor, heedless of the beauties of sky and sea, of woods and rocks, was already inspecting the beaches in search of specimens of natural history. The Assyrian, who was something of a naturalist himself, took the man of science by the hand, and led him to a great mass of rock, sloping down to the water, and thickly covered with seaweed. This place swarmed with crabs, and the Professor, whom much practice had made expert in catching these creatures, soon pulled out of its recesses as many as it was convenient for us to carry. We returned to the sloop, and putting the Professor and his prey on board, we left him to study the crabs at his leisure, and went to Bailey's Island, to which we were rowed by the Skipper, who had finished his gossip and come aboard in our absence.

Bailey's Island being several miles long, we determined to explore it and visit a store which was said to be at the other end, in order to purchase some things we needed. We therefore, on parting with the Skipper, directed him to take the sloop round to Mackerel Cove, a harbor on that side of the island toward which we proposed to walk, and be ready to take us on board in time for supper.

Our steps were first directed to a respectable looking farmhouse which had been in sight from the sloop, and had attracted our attention by its fine situation on a height near the shore, from which there could not fail to be a noble view. We wanted to see the view, to see also the people, and to get a drink of water, for our supply on the Helen had grown to be somewhat stale, and the day was warm, and our walk on Jaquiss had heated us a little.

The view we found magnificent. The people — all that were at home — consisted of two young ladies, both barefooted. The oldest, a handsome, healthy, frank-looking girl of eighteen or thereabouts, was arrayed in a dress distended by a single hoop, taken probably, as the Artist suggested, from some old barrel. The second damsel, several years younger than her sister, was reading a volume which proved to be Robinson Crusoe, a not inappropriate book for such a situation.

They received us cordially, and the younger girl ran for water to the well, which stood at some distance from the house, and was worked by an old-fashioned sweep. We sat down and had a little chat with the elder girl, whose manners were good, and her language excellent. She had visited the mainland, and had once travelled as far as Boston, but maintained, very justly, that she had seen no place so beautiful as her native island. She seemed fully to appreciate the natural loveliness of her home, and talked with discrimination of all the characteristics of the scenery.

Bidding adieu to these damsels, we walked through a grove of stately pines, and then through cultivated fields on the road toward the store.

Shortly after passing the grove we met, at the top of a long hill, a bevy of children coming home from school. We stopped them, and after they had answered some inquiries as to the road, the Assyrian pulled out a quantity of coppers which had been burning his pockets ever since he left Portland, and with impressive gravity distributed them among the urchins.

The effect of this donation was prodigious. Apparently so much money had never before been seen on Bailey's Island. The barefooted recipients, after one eager and amazed glance at their acquisitions, broke into a run, and as we watched them scudding down the long hill, we could see one after another darting into the lanes which led to their respective homes, each anxious to display his treasures to the admiring eyes of his family.

A pretty long walk brought us to the store, near which was the house of the Principal Inhabitant of the island, a retired sea-captain, renowned for his wealth and magnificence, of whom we had heard much from our female friends at the farmhouse. His abode was surrounded by appletrees, and the Principal Inhabitant himself was standing in front of it. We paid him our respects in passing, and endeavored to enter into conversation, but found it rather difficult. He would not answer a question directly, and spoke with most exasperating slowness. He had, beside, a queer habit of always turning his back to us when he said anything. We tried to circumvent him in this, by dividing our forces and surrounding him; but he was not so easily baffled. He walked to his garden fence, and, getting over, placed his back against it, and thus continued the conversation in his old attitude.

We got little out of him, however, except some opinions about the cultivation of appletrees, and the assurance, given after a slow and careful observation of the sky, that a thunderstorm was coming up, and that it would probably rain within an hour. As our own meteorological observations confirmed this prophecy, we turned our backs on the back of the Principal Inhabitant and proceeded to the store.

It was a square wooden building, painted white on one side, red on another, blue on a third, and yellow on a fourth, and contained a little of everything on the earth or beneath the earth. We made our purchases under the scrutiny of three or four of the islanders, who eyed us in silence, evidently much perplexed to reconcile our red shirts and fish-stained trousers with something in our appearance and speech that was not exactly in keeping with such garb. The Assyrian, whose long walk had made him thirsty, drew the storekeeper aside and asked if he had anything to drink. The answer was a decided negative — nothing of the kind was to be had on the island.

We departed with a sense of the efficiency of the Maine Law, and made the best of our way to Mackerel Cove, where we arrived considerably after sunset. The thunderstorm had begun, and the rain was already falling. We were very tired and hungry, and anxious to get on board the Helen, whose single mast and graceful hull were visible in the middle of the harbor. We hailed her, and after shouting for some time we saw the Skipper come on deck. He replied to our hail, but the distance was such that his answer was unintelligible. We could see, however, that the dory was absent from the sloop, and could easily conjecture that the Professor had gone on one of those untimely expeditions to which he was addicted, and had taken the Pilot with him.

Here was a predicament. But there was no help for it. We lighted our cigars, and, tired as we were, paced up and down the beach to keep ourselves warm, for it was raining hard and the air had become chilly. At length, as it was growing dark, we dimly saw at the mouth of the cove the returning boat. It grew dark so fast that we lost sight of her before she gained the sloop, but after the Professor got on board, the Skipper took the place of the Pilot, and, guided by our shouts, came for us.

In explanation of the absence of the boat, he said the Professor had been "scow-banging" — a term new to us. It meant that, as the Helen sailed into the Mackerel Cove, she passed a school of the fish from which the harbor derives its name, and the Professor, who was peculiarly fond of mackerel-fishing, had taken the Pilot and the dory and had gone in pursuit — the chase of mackerel with a boat being called by the fishermen "scow-banging." They had caught plenty, and by the time we got on board, and had changed our wet clothes for dry ones, the Pilot placed on the supper-table a heap of delicious broiled mackerel. We fell to with enthusiasm, but the Assyrian turned with disdain from the mug of tea which the Skipper set before him.

"Skipper," he said, "I am wet to the bones — nothing will dry me but whiskey. Let us have some lemonade."

The Skipper opened the locker in which the lemons were kept, and, after rummaging for some time, declared that the lemons were all gone. The last had been used in making that pail of punch for our friends of the yacht.

The Assyrian growled a little at this announcement, but at length said: "Well, well, never mind, we must do without lemons. Whiskey and hot water and sugar make a very good drink; let us have the whiskey."

The Skipper slowly produced the jug, and I saw by his face that something was the matter. He said nothing, however, but handed the vessel to the Assyrian, who placed a tumbler before him, and began to turn the jug upside down. Nothing came; it was empty. The Assyrian looked at the Skipper, and the Skipper looked at him. They understood each other without speaking. During our absence ashore, the Skipper had been entertaining some of his Swampscott friends. His hospitality was pardonable, perhaps commendable, but the consequence at that particular time and place was rather disagreeable.

"Skipper," said the Assyrian, after a time, "what is

the nearest large town on our course eastward?"

"Boothbay."

"How far is it?"

"Fifty or sixty miles."

"Can we get lemons there?"

"Certainly."

"And whiskey?"

"Very likely."

"Make sail for Boothbay as soon as it is light tomorrow. And now, Skipper, get out half a dozen bottles of ale, and let us have some clean mugs."

23

FLOUNDER FISHING
CATCHING A HALIBUT

Notwithstanding the Assyrian's impatience to
reach Boothbay, we found, when we came on deck
Friday morning, that there was little inducement to
get under way. The air was chill and damp, the sky
covered with dense clouds, and, worse than all, there
was not the slightest breath of wind. To get out of
the cove we should have to tug at the oar for at least
an hour, and on gaining the open sea might find ourselves still becalmed. So we decided to have breakfast before we started, and while that was in prepara-
tion, we dropped our lines over the side of the sloop
and caught a number of large flounders.

After breakfast a faint breeze sprang up, and,
assisted by the tide, we slowly drifted out of the
cove, and about the middle of the forenoon reached
the open sea. The wind and tide still serving, the
Skipper proposed to run southward a few miles out
of our course to Drunken Ledge and fish for halibut.
We assented, and about noon anchored in the neighborhood of a formidable reef, over which the sea
was foaming splendidly, while all around was calm
and smooth. These rocks lie in the ocean, on the

edge of Casco Bay, about five miles from the nearest islands.

Taking lines stouter and with larger hooks than those we used for cod-fishing, we baited with pieces of flounder and tried our luck. In the course of half an hour we caught several skates, large cod, haddocks, and one or two hake. But these were not what we came for, and the impatient Assyrian was already talking of Boothbay and his everlasting lemons, when suddenly a tremendous jerk, followed by a rapid rushing of the line through his fingers, put a stop to his grumbling. He had hooked a halibut at last.

"Let her run!" shouted the Pilot. "Hold tight, but don't pull her in! Let her play awhile!"

The Assyrian sprang from the bench of the cockpit where he had been reclining, and with teeth deeply set in his cigar, began to "play" his prize.

After a long and exciting contest the subdued halibut was at length brought to the surface in an exhausted condition, and was skillfully hoisted on board by the Pilot, who exclaimed, as he laid the monster on deck, "A hundred-pounder, by George!"

The delight of the Assyrian was boundless. He got upon the top of the cabin, and, swinging his hat, gave three cheers.

Then, protesting that his exertions in the struggle had made him faint and that we ought to celebrate the victory by a drink all round, he sent the Skipper into the forepeak for a bottle of ale — which order he presently countermanded for a bottle of claret, declaring that such an achievement demanded the nobler liquor. The claret was brought, and we drank to the health of the halibut, who by this time was gasping his last on deck.

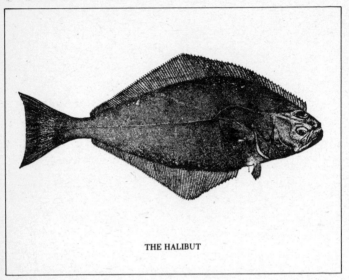

THE HALIBUT

It was truly a noble fish, lacking but a few inches of six feet in length. The body was much larger in proportion to the breadth than in its kindred, the flounder, and was dark brown on the right side, the left side being whitish. The lower jaw was longer than the upper, and both jaws were furnished with two rows of strong, sharp teeth. The lips were large and fleshy, and the eyes of remarkable size, between two and three inches in diameter.

We voted to have a piece of the halibut for dinner, for which meal the Pilot had already kindled his furnace. The Skipper accordingly cut off a huge chunk near the side fins, which he said was the best part of the fish. The Assyrian was determined that it should be cooked properly, and so he overhauled the recipes at the end of Frank Forrester's Fish and Fishing, of which we had a copy on board, till he found Soyer's recipe to boil halibut, which he read to the assembled crew, as follows:

" 'A halibut' — and this, O Pilot, applies to a piece as well as to the whole animal — 'must be well rubbed over with salt and lemon' " — here he shook his head at the Skipper — " 'before it is put in the water; have ready a large halibut-kettle — ' "

"What the deuce is a halibut-kettle?" said the Pilot.

"Never mind," said the Assyrian, "any kettle will do, if it is only big enough. Hear what comes next: 'A large halibut-kettle half full of cold water, and to every six quarts of water put one pound of salt; lay the fish in, and place it over a moderate fire; a halibut of eight pounds' — and that, Pilot, will apply to eight pounds of halibut — 'may be allowed to simmer twenty minutes, or rather more; thus it will be about three quarters of an hour altogether in the water; when it begins to crack very slightly, lift it up with the drainer and cover a clean white napkin over it; if you intend serving the sauce over your fish, dish it up with a napkin,' — hm, hm," continued the Assyrian, after a brief pause, as he ran his eye over the rest of the recipe, "I guess we may as well stop here. Let the drainer and the napkin and the sauce go. The heart of it is, Captain, you must rub it with

171

24

A STORM OFF CAPE SEGUIN
BOOTHBAY
THE COAST SURVEY SCHOONER

We sat long at table that day, and when we went
on deck about three o'clock it was raining, and the
wind was beginning to blow pretty hard. We made
sail at once in the direction of Boothbay, but in the
course of a couple of hours the wind rose to a gale.
The sea grew very rough, and almost every minute
a wave would break over our vessel and, sweeping
along the deck, deluge the cockpit with water. We
closed the cabin to keep it dry, and, gathering at the
stern, watched the sea, not without anxiety. The air
was so thick with mist that we could see nothing but
the raging waves around us, and could not tell where
we were going, though the sloop was plunging along
at a fearful rate, her bows almost continually under
water and her mast opening wide cracks at every tug
of the sails. There was considerable danger of the
mast's going overboard. In that case we should have
been completely at the mercy of the waves, on a
coast every inch of which was rock-bound, so that,
if our vessel struck, she would be pounded to pieces
in ten minutes.

We drove madly along, the grim old Pilot at the
helm, and the anxious Skipper, arrayed in oil-skin to

shed the wet, clinging to the mast and keeping a sharp lookout ahead. Suddenly the mist rose and rolled away before a sweeping blast, and then we saw Seguin lighthouse, and knew where we were. It was a superb and terrible sight — these wild reefs with the waves foaming and flashing over them, directly in our course. It was growing late, and the gale was on the increase. The sea was white with foam on the surface, but the great waves, as they came leaping and roaring at us, had a black and angry look not pleasant to behold. Our aged Pilot, as he sat clutching the helm, his hat drawn tightly over his brows to keep it from blowing off, glanced uneasily from time to time at the laboring and groaning mast, whose wide seams were alternately opening and shutting, but he said nothing. He had weathered many a harder gale, though never in so poor a craft. The Assyrian, clinging to the cover of the cabin for support, and with strong symptoms of seasickness in his face, at length broke out as a whooping billow swept over us, soaking him from head to foot:

"I say, Skipper, this is coming in rather strong. Can't we put in somewhere?"

The Skipper had been for some minutes watching a large schooner about a mile ahead of us, and, coming aft, said that it was hardly possible to weather Cape Newagin in such a storm, even if our mast held, about which he had great doubts. The schooner ahead of us was running for shelter into Sheepscut Bay, where there was an excellent harbor, and we could easily follow her in. The Pilot, after an emphatic reference to "that damned old stick," as he called the mast, assented to this opinion, and our course was accordingly changed to the northward.

Following the lead of the schooner for several miles, we reached about nightfall a beautiful and perfectly sheltered harbor, which the Skipper called sometimes Southport and sometimes Abenacook. There were a few scattered houses on the shore, but nothing that could be called a village. We anchored in the midst of a number of vessels which had, like ourselves, sought refuge there from the gale, though all except the schooner that we followed had put in earlier in the day. The storm, as we afterwards learned, raged all along the coast, and did considerable damage to the shipping.

The weather had grown so cold as to be uncomfortable even in our snug cabin, and so, after hastily swallowing some supper, we stripped off our wet clothes and turned into our berths long before our usual hour.

I lay awake half the night listening to the rain pattering on the deck, and when we arose next morning it was still pouring hard. It was so cold that the seamen got the stove out of the forepeak, and we soon had a fire in the cabin, to which the rain confined us all the forenoon. The schooner we had followed into this harbor was bound for Boothbay, and after dinner got underway and passed into Townsend Cut, a passage of some miles in length leading into Townsend Harbor, as the port of Boothbay is called. We followed, and, the rain having ceased, had a delightful sail through a most singular strait — narrow, like a river of moderate size, and bordered on both sides by meadows green to the water's edge, with occasional groves ringing the banks. We should have had no suspicion that this passage was not a river had it not been for the seaweed growing on its rocky edges.

We reached Boothbay in the course of an hour, and came to anchor a short distance off the town, which seemed to be of considerable size. The Assyrian immediately put on his shore clothes, and getting the Skipper to row him to the nearest wharf, went in search of lemons and whiskey. After a protracted absence he returned disconsolate. Lemons he had got, but whiskey was not to be obtained for love or money; the place, he said, was drier than Sahara. He brought us, however, letters and papers, so that his visit was not altogether fruitless.

As we sat reading the papers, a boat from the town came alongside with one man in it, a respectable looking person, who produced an empty bottle, and asked if we could let him have a little brandy, for which he would pay. His wife, he said was sick, and the doctor had prescribed brandy, but none was to be had in the town.

The Assyrian's sympathies were touched by this appeal, and he gave the man a couple of bottles of ale, assuring him that he would have been welcome to brandy if we had not unfortunately run out of everything of the sort. He was still expressing his admiration of the stranger's devotion when we were hailed by a boat approaching from another quarter of the town. This, too, contained a single individual, and he too produced a bottle, and, strange to say, he likewise had a sick wife, for whom the doctor had prescribed brandy.

The Assyrian's eyes began to open. "I say, my dear fellow," he remarked to the man in the boat, "are all the women in Boothbay sick, and has the doctor prescribed brandy for all of them? You're the second chap that has been here within ten minutes with the same story. Hadn't you better call a town-meeting, and confer together, so as to have a little variety in your pretenses?"

The man laughed, and explained that, as no liquor could be bought in town, the only way they had to get it was by buying it of vessels in the harbor. They had found the pretense of sickness useful in inducing their visitors to violate the law by selling to them.

Shortly after this fellow left us, the Professor, who had been studying the craft in the harbor through the telescope, pointed out a schooner at some distance which he recognized as the United States Coast-Survey vessel, the Hassler, and said he knew one of her officers.

The Assyrian snapped his fingers in delight. "I know one too," he said, "and a right good fellow he is. Let us go on board. We shall find something there to wet our whistles with, I know."

In a few minutes we were all in the dory, and the

Skipper rowed us alongside the schooner. We were cordially received by the three officers on board, and found the Assyrian's prediction amply verified. As we sat in the cabin, whose spaciousness seemed magnificent compared with that of the Helen, I was startled by the sudden appearance at my elbow of an ebony complexioned individual, bearing a tray containing decanters, glasses, lemons, and a pitcher of hot water. How he had got into the cabin was inconceivable, for he certainly had not descended by the only visible entrance. His coming, so sudden and so noiseless, made me think of the genie of the lamp that waited on Aladdin. But though he came in so questionable a manner, "the prince of darkness was a gentleman." Placing the tray before us, he vanished as silently as he came — behind a curtain.

We spent a merry evening, and on parting, our friends of the Hassler invited us to dine with them on board the schooner next day, remarking, by way of enticement, that their steward had been to market that afternoon, and had brought back a fine leg of veal. We accepted the invitation, and got back to the sloop a little before midnight. To celebrate the discovery of the Hassler, we fired off, before we turned in, all our remaining rockets, blue-lights, and Roman candles.

The next morning (Sunday) was serene and mild. After breakfast, two of the officers of the Hassler came to visit us in their cutter, and the Assyrian proposed that, as we were going for the first time in several weeks to have a Christian dinner, we should all go to church. To this reasonable proposal we agreed, and, dressing ourselves in our best clothes, went ashore in man-of-war style with the United States officers. After rambling awhile on the beach, we went in search of a meeting-house. A very deaf old fellow, whom we made to understand by much shouting what we wanted, conducted us to a sort of garret, where we found a small and singularly hard-favored congregation, who greeted our entrance with a stare which was prolonged throughout the whole service. Presently the minister entered, and he too fixed his eyes upon us as we sat in a row on a back bench, and seldom removed his gaze, except when he shut his eyes to pray.

It was a Methodist meeting, and notwithstanding the homeliness of the place and the people, the sermon was sound discourse, full of practical good sense. The Assyrian listened with devout attention, and, when we came out, declared that he could now eat the fatted calf with a good conscience. Re-embarking in the cutter, we were soon on board the Hassler, where dinner was speedily served by the mysterious gentleman in black, who came and went in the most absolute silence.

After dinner, we adjourned with our cigars to the deck, and spent the afternoon in conversation, which was prolonged by jest and story far into the evening. Tea was served on deck, soon after sunset, by the speechless African, whose silence to this day I know not whether to ascribe to absolute dumbness or to his sense of discipline.

as we swept by. The mackerel, as usual, excited the Professor, and he invited me to jump into the dory with him, and go and catch a mess for breakfast, for which meal the Pilot was leisurely making preparations. The wind was so light that the smoke of our furnace ascended like the smoke of a sacrifice, straight up, and at the rate at which the sloop was going we could easily overtake her. As we were now getting fairly into the region of mackerel-fishing, the Skipper had taken care to provide bait, which he purchased from a vessel with a bait-mill on board.

Taking a bucket of the stuff, composed of hardheads ground up, we entered the dory and rowed toward the nearest school — its presence being easily detected by the ripple which the fishes make in passing through the water. When within two or three rods of them, the Professor dropped the oars and threw several handfuls of the bait toward the mackerel. Our lines were already baited with pieces of hardhead, and we threw them quickly out. Instantly there was a rush at them, a sharp, quick bite, and we each pulled in a mackerel. For a few minutes we drew in fish as fast as we could bait and throw out our lines; often, indeed, not stopping to put on fresh bait, for the merest shred of skin hanging to the hook was sufficient. We had caught about thirty in quick succession, the fish following as our boat floated along on the tide, when suddenly they ceased to bite. Something had alarmed them, and they had gone off like a flash to reappear at the distance of an eighth of a mile. As we had already more than enough for breakfast, we did not pursue them, but regained the sloop and turned our captures over to the Pilot, who soon had the choicest of them in his frying pan.

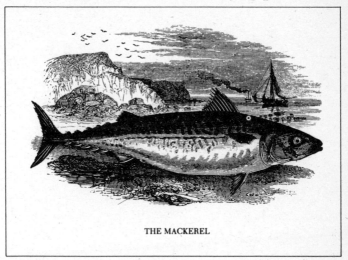

THE MACKEREL

This was my first experience of mackerel-fishing, and very pleasant I found it. I have not yet seen any fish so handsome as the mackerel, so elegant in form, so beautiful and brilliant in color. The upper part of the body is dark green in hue, the lower part silvery white, but along the sides are wavy bands of mixed and fluctuating colors like those of silk. The size of the fish varies from ten to twenty inches in length, and the average weight is two pounds. Those we caught were small, weighing not more than a pound each.

Before the Revolution, the mackerel fishery was largely prosecuted on the coast of New England by sloops fitted out for the purpose, of which Massachusetts had about a hundred. Afterward, this branch of industry decayed, and for a considerable period boats only were used. But about the beginning of this century, a vessel was sent to Mount Desert to catch mackerel, and made so profitable a trip that the business soon revived, and became more prosperous than ever. At present, about 1,000 vessels and 5,000 seamen from Massachusetts are employed in mackerel fishing, and, beside the numbers of the fish which are sold to be eaten fresh, nearly 300,000 barrels are annually inspected in Massachusetts, which are worth about $1,500,000. The salted mackerel are sold chiefly in the Slave States, but a large proportion of the poorer quality is exported to South America, and to the East and West Indies.

When a mackerel vessel reaches a place where the fish are supposed to be plentiful, the master furls all his sails except the mainsail, brings his vessel's bow to the wind, ranges his crew at intervals along one of her sides, and, without a mackerel in sight, attempts to raise a school by throwing over bait. The baiter stands amidships, with the bait-box outside the rail, and with a tin cup nailed to a long handle, he scatters the bait on the water. If the mackerel appear, the men throw out short lines, to the hooks of which a glittering pewter jig is affixed. The fish, if they bite at all, generally bite rapidly, and are hauled in as fast as the most active man can throw out and draw in a line. As they pull them on board, the fisherman, with a jerk, throws the fish into a barrel standing beside him. So ravenously do they bite, that sometimes a barrelful is caught in fifteen minutes by a single man. Some active young men will haul in and jerk off a fish and throw out the line for another with a single motion, and repeat the act in so rapid succession that their arms seem continually on the swing.

Sometimes, after thousands have been caught by the ten or twelve men of the crew, the mackerel suddenly disappear. The lines are then thrown aside, and all hands go to work to dress the fish, the captain or mate first counting them, and noting down in the fish-book what each man has caught. The mackerel are split and cleaned, and soaked awhile in barrels of salt water. They are then washed and handed to the salter, who puts a handful of salt in the bottom of a barrel, takes a fish in his right hand, rolls it in salt, and places it skin downward in the barrel, till he comes to the top layer, which is placed skins up and well covered with salt. When the vessel returns to port, the fish are sent on shore to be sorted into three or four qualities, weighed, re-packed, re-salted, and re-pickled.

The mackerel fishery, as pursued by the New Englanders, is a toilsome and perilous calling, and success in it can only be achieved by great energy and activity. It is carried on chiefly in schooners, averaging fifty tons, which follow their prey to the Gulf of St. Lawrence, and even to the bleak and stormy coast of Labrador.

26

The breeze freshened as we gained the open
sea, and though the swell was very rough from the
recent storm, we swept along delightfully through
a host of islands, fair to look upon, though not pos-
sessing the romantic beauty of the isles of Casco
Bay. This part of the coast of Maine is interesting
from its legendary and historical associations. We
passed in the course of the forenoon the Island of
Monhegan, which comprises a thousand acres of
good land, well cultivated by about a hundred inhabitants, a remarkably intelligent and prosperous
people, who form a pure democracy and manage
their public business entirely without officers of
any kind, their only public edifice being a schoolhouse, which serves on Sundays for a church.

Close to Monhegan is an islet called Mananas,
on a rocky ledge, in the center of which was discovered in 1808 an inscription in characters supposed to be Runic. If the Vinland of the Norsemen
was in New England, there can be no doubt that
those bold searovers must have lingered long and
lovingly on this coast of Maine, which so much resembles that of their own Norway, with its deep

fiords, its rocky isles, and its sea-washed mountains.
At all events, it pleased my fancy to imagine the
adventurous Biorn and his companions sailing along
the track we were pursuing, gazing with wondering
eyes on the same islands and headlands, unchanged
in any material aspect by the lapse of a thousand
years.

The earliest attempts of the English at coloniz-
ing New England were made here early in the

MONHEGAN ISLAND

seventeenth century by Sir Ferdinando Gorges. Captain John Smith visited Monhegan in 1614, and a
settlement was made on the island in 1618, two
years before the Pilgrims arrived at Plymouth. A
little farther to the eastward, on the island of Mount
Desert, the mission of St. Saviour had been founded
in 1613 by the French Jesuit, Father Pierre Baird,
and destroyed, together with other French settle-
ments in Maine, by Sir Samuel Argal of Virginia.
At a later period, the adventurous Baron de St. Cas-
tine came from Canada and built a fortress on the
site of the town which now bears his name. He mar-

187

ried the daughter of the great Modocawando, the most powerful sachem of the East, and had a wild and romantic career till his castle was taken and plundered by Sir Edmund Andros, Governor of Massachusetts.

OWL'S HEAD

The breeze being fair and steady, we held on our course without stopping, till, at 6 p.m., we reached Owl's Head, an exceedingly picturesque promontory where a large white lighthouse crowned a high rock rising abruptly from the water. Here we anchored in a broad channel between the mainland and two islands, amid a fleet of vessels. This channel is much frequented by coasters and fishermen, and five hundred sails have been seen passing Owl's Head in one day.

After supper the Assyrian persuaded the Artist and me to go ashore and walk with him to the large town of Rockland, where he was assured by the Skipper that whiskey could be obtained without fail. To make a proper impression on the people of that place, he arrayed himself in his best attire, putting on a fashionable stove-pipe hat which he had carefully reserved for a great emergency. In spite of his pleadings, we wore our red shirts, fishy trousers, and old felt hats, and consequently made rather a rowdy appearance by the side of the Assyrian.

We set off at a good pace. The distance to Rockland, according to the Skipper, being only three miles, and the weather fine though growing cold, we were highly pleased at the prospect of stretching our legs after being cramped up in the little sloop. We went on cheerfully for perhaps a couple of miles, on a road bordered by woods, till we met a man driving a wagon on his way to Owl's Head. We stopped and asked:

"Is this the road to Rockland?"

"Wal, it is."

"How far is it?"

"Wal, a little mor'n three miles."

The wagoner drove on, leaving us not very well satisfied. We kept on, however, for about a mile farther, where we encountered a traveller on foot who assured us that Rockland was still about three miles distant. The distance was evidently diminishing, and we pushed vigorously onward, till at length, after walking about five miles, we reached the town of which we were in search, about 9 p.m. To our surprise, it proved to be a handsome, city-like place, with well-built brick blocks and granite sidewalks. The whole population appeared to be in the street, returning, as we learned, from a brass-band concert.

The Assyrian directed his steps to a hotel, where he asked about the fluid resources of the town. The answer was discouraging. Nothing stronger than beer was to be had for love or money. Unwilling to credit so fearful a state of destitution in a place of such size and apparent business, our thirsty friend went forth to explore, leaving us to read the newspapers and gather the news of the last few weeks. In about half an hour he returned tolerably successful. He had found, at a druggists', several bottles of Wolfe's Aromatic Schiedam Schnapps, which, in spite of its pretensions to be medicine, he said was really a pretty good article of gin, though abominably diluted with water. Still, it was fit for drink, and, in the absence of better liquor, might be endured.

We set out at once on our return, each alternately bearing the precious package, which was confoundedly heavy. We reached Owl's Head just at midnight, scarcely able to stand, we were so fatigued from want of practice in walking. The weather had changed greatly in the course of the evening. It had grown quite cold, and the clouds indicated speedy rain. With some difficulty we detected the Helen amid a crowd of vessels of all sizes. The Assyrian hailed her:

"Hallo! the Helen, the Helen ahoy!"

There was no response. In fact, all on board were sound asleep, having turned in under the impression that we should stay at Rockland all night. The Assyrian hailed again repeatedly, and with the utmost force of his lungs, and we joined him in the outcry. There was still no answer from the sloop, but men on board other vessels halloed at us in wrath for making such a disturbance, and dogs on the shore set up a furious barking. There was evidently no use in attempting to rouse our sleeping friends. We walked about the village for a while, seeking a tavern. None was to be seen. At length, growing desperate with fatigue and cold, we tried to raise the inmates of several dwellings in succession, but without effect; we could not waken a soul. There must be something peculiarly sleep-provoking in the atmosphere of Owl's Head, for we made din enough to rouse the dead.

Our next effort was in search of a boat. We prowled in the dark and the rain for some distance along the shore. We found only two skiffs, one of which was full of water, and the other was moored beyond our reach except by swimming. We turned again to the village, and found at length a ruinous cooper-shop, in which we took refuge from the rain, and made an attempt to sleep. With a stick of wood for a pillow, we lay down on a pile of shavings, and for a few minutes slumbered; but the cold wind blew so keenly through the chasms in the walls of the hut, that we soon woke, and were forced to rise and move about to keep warm. At length it occurred to me that the schoolhouse of the village would probably afford us a comfortable shelter, if we could find it. We remembered enough of the feats of our schoolboy days to be confident that we could get into any building of the sort in New England.

As the rain had somewhat abated, we sallied forth and happily in a few minutes found the building which we sought — a house of one story with a single chimney, windows high above the ground, and no fence around it. After scouting it carefully, we assisted the Assyrian to clamber up to a window which had fortunately been left a little open. That gentleman, after much effort, at last got his knee upon the windowsill, and, pushing up the sash, thrust in his head.

At this moment two or three quick screams and outcries — "Thieves! murder! help!" — evidently from a female voice — broke upon our horrified ears. They were followed by a rough voice demanding with an oath what we wanted. It was no time for explanations. And in fact none were needed by us. We had mistaken a dwelling for a schoolhouse, and were breaking into a bedroom — that was all. The Assyrian let go the sash, which, in its descent, struck off his new hat, which fell of course within the room. He then dropped himself to the ground, and we all ran away as fast as we could.

We again took refuge in the cooper's shop, congratulating ourselves that it was not the fashion on the coast of Maine to sleep with pistols under the pillow, and wondering at the taste which led people to build their dwellings in the same fashion that they did their schoolhouses. We made another attempt to sleep in the shavings, but the cold still kept us awake. We therefore descended to the shore again, and, after long walking on the beach, found a boat with oars, which some fisherman had left ready to go out in to his daily task at dawn. We took the liberty of borrowing it, and were soon on board the sloop. Stopping merely to wake the Skipper and send him back with the borrowed boat, we turned into our berths, and, wrapped in warm blankets, were soon oblivious of all our troubles.

27

FIRE AND WATER
PULPIT HARBOR
THE CUSK   A STRANGE FISH

The Professor and the two seamen, who had
had their natural share of sleep while the rest of
us were wandering in the cold and darkness of Owl's
Head, rose at four in the morning and got the sloop
under way while we yet slept. The wind at starting
was moderate, but in the course of an hour it had
risen to a gale, accompanied by squalls of rain and
mist, which made the air so thick that the land was
totally hidden from sight, and the pilot could not
tell where to steer. The pitching of the vessel in the
heavy sea aroused me a little after five. Leaving
the Artist and the Assyrian asleep in their berths, I
went on deck. The only object in sight beside the
white waves and the driving clouds that enveloped
us, was a schooner ahead, pursuing the same course
with ourselves. We were at the entrance to Penob-
scott Bay, six or seven miles from the mainland.

We followed the schooner for a mile or two,
and at length caught sight of land at no great distance, which proved to be Fox Island.* The schooner

*Now called North Haven, while its sister island is Vinal-
haven.

194

kept close to the shore, and presently disappeared from our view within a narrow opening in the rocky coast, which we now dimly perceived. It was a harbor not on the charts, and unknown to our seamen, but they said that if the schooner had got in we could of course follow, and it was not advisable to keep the sea in such a storm with our unsound mast. The Pilot, who by this time had got his great iron furnace ablaze with coals, ready for cooking breakfast, now steered for the entrance of the harbor, which was very narrow, with a huge black rock rising right in the middle.

This narrow channel was so strikingly picturesque that I went below to wake the Artist and the Assyrian, leaving the Skipper and the Professor standing at the bow and looking out sharply for reefs and rocks, of which they occasionally gave notice to the Pilot. I had succeeded, by considerable shaking and punching, in restoring the sleepers to a glimmering of consciousness, when a tremendous uproar on deck called me to the companion-way to see what the matter was.

A terrible and yet laughable sight met my eyes. As the sloop was surging into the entrance of the harbor, the Skipper discovered a sunken reef right ahead of the vessel. He shouted to the Pilot to put his helm up, and the Professor ran aft to assist in shifting the boom. Before he could reach the stern a squall struck the sloop, and the boom, as it swung over, hit the Professor, who, to save himself, clung to the spar and was carried half over the side of the vessel. At the same time, the boom knocked off the Pilot's hat. To this particular article of apparel the old man had a special attachment, generated probably by the years it had crowned his head. He therefore with one hand made a desperate grab at the hat, which he caught, while with the other he pushed out the boom, to which the Professor was still hanging, with his heels clinging to the rail of the vessel. The Pilot, at the same time, gave a great kick at the tiller to put it hard up, but missed it and hit his furnace, which toppled over. The glowing coals fell into a basket of shavings and kindlings under the bench, which runs around the cockpit, and these highly combustible materials immediately blazed up. Other coals set fire to the dry space beneath the bench, where the rain never penetrated; others yet, falling upon the wet deck, caused a great gushing up of steam and smoke.

This was the state of affairs when I stuck my head out of the cabin, followed by the half-asleep Artist and Assyrian. The flame and smoke and steam that whirled in our faces, together with the howling of the storm and the frowning look of the black rock that guards the mouth of the harbor, to which we were so close that it seemed right over our heads, were well calculated to give a slight shock to our nerves. Such sudden and unexpected dangers were really exciting, though we could not help laughing at the droll attitudes into which the boom had knocked our friends.

There being several buckets at hand, and our

vessel so low in the water that we could fill them by merely leaning over the side, the fire was easily got under control. The sloop glided past the reef, whose presence in the way had caused the commotion, and which she cleared with a slight touch without damage; we sailed into the harbor and presently were in still water.

This harbor is called Pulpit Harbor, from the great, high, isolated rock at the entrance, which the church-going New Englanders have likened to a pulpit, as in the case of so many other "pulpit-rocks" on their coast. It is one of the finest havens I ever saw, if not the very finest. Except the narrow entrance it was land-locked, and as calm and sheltered as an inland pond. Its diameter seemed to be about half a mile, and it was surrounded by low hills sloping gently to the water's edge. The summits of the hills were covered with woods, but on their cleared and grassy slopes cattle and sheep were pasturing. A few fishermen's houses were in sight, and beside the schooner we had followed in, there were half a dozen small fishing vessels at anchor in front of the hamlet.

We anchored in the middle of the harbor, just opposite the entrance, through which we had a view of the turbulent sea outside. The storm, however, was abating, the rain had ceased, and by the time we had finished breakfast the sun broke from the clouds. Nowhere, I am sure, did it smile on a lovelier or more peaceful scene. Nothing could exceed the exquisite freshness of the hillsides, and the groves that bounded the landward view were a tasteful and natural frame to the picture. Seaward, we looked as through some mighty portal, over the black and jagged rocks of the entrance, and thence across ten miles of ocean to the mainland, where the picturesque Camden Mountains reared their summits in full view. These mountains are not far from the shore, and form a remarkably beautiful range, rising to the height of fifteen hundred feet above the surrounding plain. They lie directly opposite the entrance to Pulpit Harbor.

To complete the charm of the landscape, a number of large fish-hawks, whose huge nests we could see on the branches of a grove of tall pines, were wheeling high in the air with their wings extended and apparently motionless, watching a school of mackerel near Pulpit Rock, and occasionally descending and seizing fishes, which they carried to their nests, uttering as they went fierce screams of triumph and delight.

About the middle of the forenoon the Assyrian remembered the schnapps he had purchased at Rockland. He looked around the cabin for it, but the package was nowhere visible. He examined the lockers and poked about the forepeak. It was not to be found. Proceeding to the deck, he hailed the skipper, who was just going ashore for water, and had already got a few strokes of his oars from the sloop, and asked him what he had done with the schnapps?

"Schnapps," repeated the Skipper, slowly backing water, and evidently wondering what scrape he had got into now. "I don't know anything about schnapps. There hasn't been any schnapps on board."

The Assyrian hung down his head as if lost in thought. At last he spoke: "I remember now — I left the package in that infernal cooper's shop at Owl's Head. The fates are against me. I shall drink water for the rest of the cruise." And stepping into the dory to avoid our gibes, he told the Skipper he would go with him to the nearest spring, and make trial of his new beverage.

While they were absent, we got out our lines and fished. The water was very deep and fish abundant. We caught cod, haddock, whiting, skate, and a large Greenland sculpin, a handsome monster with a dark-brown back, and sides and belly adorned with circular spots of yellow and white.

A fish resembling a hake, of which we caught several, the largest thirty inches in length and five pounds in weight, the Pilot called a cusk. The liver, he said, was full of oil of a kind good for burns. We had the cusk cooked for dinner, and found its flesh firm to toughness, but savory enough. When salted, the Pilot said, some people preferred it to cod, as the flesh swells much in boiling, and divides into thick flakes.

The Skipper and the Assyrian not having returned when dinner was nearly ready, we sounded the horn to recall them. They obeyed the summons, and during dinner the Assyrian described the beauties of North Fox Island, while he declared to be

199

the finest he had yet seen. A winding strait about a mile broad separates it from South Fox Island. This strait is called the Thoroughfare, and coasters and fishing-vessels often pass through it. The island was well stocked with sheep, and the flowers were peculiarly brilliant in hue from the effect of sea air. The Assyrian had talked with some of the people, who lived, he said, in very good houses. He had learned that the island formed the town of North Haven; that it contained eight hundred inhabitants, four small villages, as many stores, one church, and eleven school-houses; and, lastly, that its staple product was hay. The only natural curiosity was a huge rocking-boulder, on the top of a hill adjoining Pulpit Harbor.

After dinner, the Artist and I went with the Professor in the dory to dredge near the mouth of the harbor. Before we began, the beauty of the seaweeds on a ledge nearby attracted our attention, and we landed on the rocks and gathered a great quantity of them.

The result of our dredging was a few fine specimens of sea-cucumbers, the largest we had yet seen.

About the middle of the afternoon a great school of mackerel came into the harbor. We all got into the dory, except the seamen, and anchored alongside of Pulpit Rock, to intercept them as they came out. Our bait, which we threw out by handfuls, soon attracted them, and a lively scene ensued. For about half an hour we pulled in mackerel as fast as we could throw out and haul in our lines. After catching upward of a hundred, we stopped, as we really did not know what to do with the fish, and did not care to capture them merely to throw back into the sea.

A thunderstorm confined us to the sloop for the rest of the day. Before sundown it cleared up, and as the setting sun descended directly behind the opposite mountains, we were favored with a strange and magnificent spectacle. After the storm the sky had become perfectly clear of clouds, except a dense mass that rested on the mountain peaks. As the sun went down, these clouds gathered around the summit of Magunticook, the loftiest peak of the mountains, and assumed the form of a crown, which was presently suffused and glorified with a rich rosy hue. For nearly half an hour this superb circlet remained motionless on the brow of the mountain, till it gradually melted away as the shades of evening advanced.

Before the twilight vanished we began to fish, as the Professor thought we might find the place abundant in hake. In a few minutes I hauled up a lobster, in whose tail my hook had somehow got fast. It was in fine condition, and weighed twelve pounds. As we had been for some days without lobster, the unlucky crustacean went at once into the Pilot's pot.

We were catching whiting pretty freely, when, just as it was growing dark, an exclamation of surprise from the Assyrian called us to his side. He had caught what we at first supposed to be a conger-eel.

But it proved to be a fish of the sculpin family, and of an entirely new and strange species. It was so queer and savage-looking that none of us ventured to touch it or take it from the hook. We inspected and measured it while the Assyrian held it at arm's length. Its body was shaped like that of an eel, but its head was square and blunt, with an almost human face. It had a steady, stony expression in its deep-set eyes. Its length was thirty inches, and its circumference eight inches. But its most remarkable peculiarity was its color, which was a ghastly white except at the tail, where it shaded into a rosy hue.

There is no fish like this described by any writer on ichthyology, and none of us had ever seen anything of the sort before. The Pilot, who had fished in our waters for more than half a century, declared that he had never seen or heard of such a creature in all his experience. On turning in that night, we left our baited lines hanging over the vessel's side, and in the morning found we had caught a fish resembling the other in everything, except that it was of a lead color instead of white.

28

I went on deck before sunrise next morning, to see how Pulpit Harbor looked at that hour. The weather was clear and mild, and the Megunticook peaks were tipped with the rosy hues of dawn, while we lay still in deep shadow. I found the Pilot sitting on the taffrail, pipe in mouth, and absorbed in the study of the bewildering inscriptions on a package of yeast-powder which he had bought in Portland. He was evidently planning some great stroke of culinary art. By much severe scrutiny and some muttered spelling, he at last mastered the directions on the package, and proceeded to open it with the air of a man who knew what he was about. I ventured to inquire what was in the wind. He answered, with his usual brevity and directness, "Flapjacks."

By the time the flapjacks were mixed and the frying pan ready, we were all on deck and intently observing the process of preparing them. The old man poured a quantity of the batter into his pan, which was already sizzling with fat, and when the huge cake was sufficiently done, proceeded to turn it with a knife. He did not succeed very well in this difficult operation, and the Assyrian said:

"That's a lubberly way of doing it, Uncle Widger. You should loosen the flapjack with your knife, and then, taking the frying pan in your hand, throw the flapjack into the air in such a way that it will turn a somersault and come down soft side into the pan. That's the way to turn flapjacks."

"I should like to see you do it," said the old man.

"Do it!" said the confident Assyrian; "I can do it as easy as I can eat the flapjack after it is done. Here, let me take your knife and I'll show you the trick."

He carefully loosened the flapjack from the bottom of the pan, and then, seizing the handle with both hands, he tossed up the frying pan with considerable force, giving at the same time a scientific twist to his wrists for the purpose of making the flapjack turn over in the air, while he stood ready to catch it. Unluckily, this last flourish was not successful. The flapjack, instead of falling perpendicularly, went with a slant over the stern into the sea.

The discomfited Assyrian made no attempt to try again, but silently handed back the frying pan to the Pilot, and took refuge in the cabin. The mirth of the old man at his instructor's failure was pleasant to behold. He laughed and chuckled with infinite glee, and though he made great efforts to suppress his merriment and preserve a sober aspect, his delight ran over perpetually at his eyes and would break out every few minutes into a sudden roar. It was not till breakfast was over, and we had made sail and got out of the harbor and on the open sea, that he resumed his usual gravity.

Our course was northeast, toward Deer Island, on the eastern side of Penobscot Bay. This island is ten miles long by five miles broad, and has two or three thousand inhabitants. We sailed for several

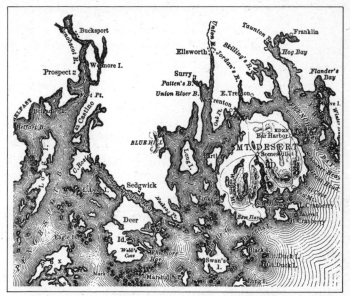

hours through a group of smaller islands, steering for a channel which ran between Deer Island and Little Deer Island, and communicated with Edgemoggin Reach. On reaching the spot indicated on the chart as a navigable strait, we found it, to our astonishment, dry land, and were forced to come to anchor near a number of fishing vessels which, like ourselves, had apparently been caught in this trap.

We learned that the strait was passable only at high water, and, while waiting for the tide to rise, the Professor and the Assyrian went out in the dory to dredge, while the Artist and I rambled over the rocky bottom of the channel through which our vessel was to sail into Edgemoggin Reach. It was a broad, irregular ravine, worn apparently by the action of the water, and its high, rocky shores were honey-combed with caves and gullies. Behind a huge promontory, at which our stroll terminated, we found a dozen young ladies arrayed in trousers and long leather boots, hard at work digging clams, which they put into baskets and carried on their shoulders to a large scow lying in the mud not far off.

They were a lively set of damsels, and had a pleasant habit of playing practical jokes upon each other of rather a rough sort. We amused ourselves by watching their gambols and their labors, until the rising tide obliged them to desist from work. After a smart skirmish, in which their baskets and handfuls of mud were freely used as missiles, they embarked in their scow and rowed away, with a parting remark to us to go home to our anxious mothers in time for tea.

At 2 p.m. it was high tide, and the Skipper, who had been on shore seeking a pilot, came on board with one of the Deer Islanders, a queer-looking fellow, who had offered for half a dollar to navigate the sloop through the channel. We hoisted sail immediately, and with a boisterous wind, were soon scudding over the places on which I had walked dry-shod but a few hours before. It was a perilous passage. There was little enough water anywhere, and the channel was broken by huge patches of rock, some sunken and others rising to the surface. Our new pilot gave himself wholly up to the contemplation of a heap of sea-cucumbers, the fruit of the Professor's dredging, which lay on deck. He was very talkative when he first came on board, but the moment his eyes lighted on these strange animals he was struck dumb with astonishment. He fell on his hands and knees before the heap, which he scrutinized in every possible way, by handling, smelling, and touching with his tongue. Meantime we were running at a furious rate amid rocks and shoals, which the old Pilot at the helm was avoiding as best he could, until the anxious Skipper, forgetting in alarm for our safety his habitual politeness, touched the new comer with his foot, and told him to get up and mind his business.

He rose reluctantly to his feet, his eyes still fixed on the sea-cucumbers, exclaiming, "Lor-a-mighty, what'll ye do with them?"

"Cook 'em," said the Assyrian, who had been eying the fellow with intense disgust, "and if we get on the rocks we'll cook you. So you had better look sharp."

The hint was taken, and the islander, withdrawing his gaze from the sea-cucumbers, glanced at the surrounding waters, and gave to our old Pilot some directions how to steer. Here a new difficulty arose. The old man did not understand the terms used by the newcomer, and for a while great confusion and uproar raged on the sloop, which seemed likely to end only in her going to pieces on the rocks. The two pilots grew angry and excited, and bawled their wrath at each other from opposite ends of the vessel, till the Skipper took upon himself the part of interpreter.

For a little while everything went well enough, till the irresistible sea-cucumbers again attracted the islander's attention. Quitting his post at the bow, he ran to the heap, and fell again on his knees to examine them, asking, at the same time, a volley of incoherent questions. The irritated Skipper, seizing him by the arm, led him back to the bow, where he talked to him earnestly for a minute or two, and then came aft to the cockpit where we were all gathered. "The fellow's as drunk as a loon," he whispered to us through his teeth. "I didn't find it out till just now. 'Twill be a wonder if we ever get safe into the Reach with such a chap for pilot."

Here was a pleasant prospect, truly! The wind was blowing almost a gale, and, as we knew by our own examination while the tide was out, the channel through which we were passing abounded with reefs and shoals. The soberest pilot would have found it hard enough to guide a vessel through, and we were trusting to the skill of a drunken loafer, whose wits at best were evidently none of the brightest or steadiest. To do the fellow justice, however, he did know the channel perfectly, and we got at last safely into Edgemoggin Reach, a broad sound running for several miles between Deer Island and the mainland. With this sound our seamen were well acquainted, and beside, we had a good chart of it, so that we needed no further pilotage.

There was something in the aspect of the Deer Islander which strongly excited the ire of the Assyrian, who stepped up to him as he was about to get into the dory to be rowed ashore by the Skipper. Taking him gently by the throat, he solemnly warned him never again to undertake, while drunk, to act as a pilot, assuring him that he had run a very close chance of being flung overboard, and might not, on a second occasion, escape so easily. He gave him a few shakes to settle this advice in his memory, and then politely assisted him into the dory, which the Skipper was holding alongside.

We lay-to till the Skipper returned, and then made a splendid run down Edgemoggin Reach which, from one end to the other, was white with foam. There cannot be a finer sheet of water in the world than this Reach, which is bounded on every side by superb views. Far before us, on the right, rose the blue summit of Isle Haut, as the early French navigators named it — a mountain rising from the waves. Before us the peaks of Mount Desert came gradually into view, at first misty and blue, then green and wooded, until, as we advanced, still loftier summits showed themselves in grim and stony desolation.

GREAT HEAD, MOUNT DESERT

29

MOUNT DESERT
AN UNBENDING LANDLORD
END OF THE CRUISE

The approach to Mount Desert by sea is magnificent. The island is a mass of mountains crowded together, and seemingly rising from the water. As you draw near, they resolve themselves into thirteen distinct peaks, the highest of which is about two thousand feet above the neighboring ocean. It is difficult to conceive of any finer combination of land and water than this view. Certainly only in the tropics can it be excelled — only in the gorgeous islands of the Indian and Pacific Oceans. On the coast of America it has no rival, except, perhaps, at the Bay of Rio de Janeiro.

None of us knew anything of Mount Desert, and we therefore put into the first harbor that we saw on the coast, which proved to be Bass Harbor. We landed about sunset, and, not finding the village very attractive, the Assyrian, the Artist, and I started for Southwest Harbor, which was described to us as the place of most resort on the island. The Professor, wishing to dredge in these waters, preferred to remain on board with the seamen, promising to bring the sloop around to Southwest Harbor next day.

We could not obtain at Bass Harbor any conveyance, all the horses of the place being absent on some rustic excursion. So we walked through the forest for several miles, after dark, and for the last hour of the way had a fine night-view of the mountains, serene and solemn in the starlight. About 11 p.m. we reached our destination — a public house, had been recommended to us at Bass Harbor. We were cold, hungry, and exceedingly tired, and our hearts sank as we saw that no light was visible, and that apparently everybody had gone to bed.

"If they sleep here as soundly as they do at Owl's Head," said the Assyrian, as he pounded the front door with his fist, "our prospects of going to bed supperless may be pronounced first-rate. At all events, I give you fair notice I shall attempt no more schoolhouses."

Our fears were groundless. The landlord speedily appeared, having fortunately just got into bed as we began to knock. He took us into the kitchen, which was tolerably warm, and produced some cold meat and applepie. The Assyrian, considering the cruise at an end as soon as we landed on Mount Desert, had already taken back his pledge of abstinence made at Pulpit Harbor, and was desirous of warming himself with something more heating than water. He therefore meekly asked the landlord if he couldn't give us something to drink.

The landlord smiled, and suggested milk.

"I have a weak stomach," said the Assyrian, "and never drink anything so strong as milk."

The landlord smiled still more blandly, and his smile expanded into a slight laugh as he proposed cold tea.

"Bah!" said the disgusted Assyrian. "Why don't you offer us dishwater at once? Can't you give us some whiskey?"

"No."

"Brandy?"

"No."

"Ale? — cider?"

"No, nothing of the kind."

The landlord was inflexible, and we went to bed in a state of the most perfect sobriety.

Next morning after breakfast, we hired of the landlord a one-horse wagon and a quiet-looking beast of a mare, to convey us to Bar Harbor on the northeast side of the island, which we had learned was the best place to stop at, if we desired to be near the finest scenery. A drive of several miles over a rough mountain road brought us to Somesville, a village at the head of a broad sound which runs up from the ocean several miles. Here we dined at the house of a publican, who was also a sinner. Being a Democrat, he held the Maine Law at defiance, and openly violated it, though he had been repeatedly threatened with prosecutions.

After dinner, we drove for several miles through a forest where nothing living was visible but squirrels, rabbits, partridges, and an occasional eagle soaring overhead. We passed no house nor sign of human handiwork, except a ruined mill, near which, as we descended a steep hill, the harness of our wagon broke. The mare, which up to this moment had been the most amiable of animals, now displayed a frightful perversity. After a vigorous attempt to run away, which was baffled by turning her head into the bushes that lined the road, she suddenly stood stock still, and began kicking with her hind legs, with a force, precision, and rapidity that resembled more the working of a powerful machine than anything of the animal nature. It was admirable to witness, but extremely inconvenient to be near. In a minute the front part of the wagon was dashed to splinters, and the Artist and I were both badly bruised. We jumped out, and succeeded in quieting the mare, though not till the harness was broken in a dozen places.

As we were yet three or four miles from Bar Harbor, and we had not a bit of cord or string with which to mend the harness, we found ourselves in something of a dilemma. Just at this moment a wagon approached from the direction of Bar Harbor. There were two men in it, who stopped as they came to the scene of our disaster. The Assyrian uttered a shout, and sprang forward with outstretched hands. They were classmates of his, whom he had not seen since he left college years before, and whom he least of all expected to meet on a lonely road in the heart of the hills of Mount Desert.

The meeting was exceedingly fortunate. They were guests at Bar Harbor, whither we were bound, and they were now on their way to a lake high up among the mountains, to fish for trout. With the aid of their lines we repaired the harness, and parting from our friends, who promised to bring us a mess of trout for supper, made our way without further delay to Bar Harbor. There we found excellent

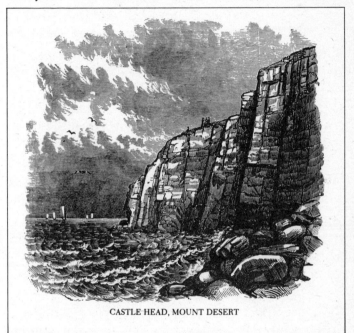

CASTLE HEAD, MOUNT DESERT

quarters in the house of Mr. Roberts, the postmaster and principal trader of the village. At this place we spent two days exploring the recesses of Otter Creek, whose wild mountain-passes equal in grandeur the Notch of the White Hills,* and rambling about the gigantic cliffs of Great Head, Schooner Head, and

---

*Crawford Notch.

the other bold rocky promontories rising for hundreds of feet directly from the sea, which make the island so fascinating to the landscape and marine painter.

Mount Desert has an area of about a hundred square miles, and is divided into three towns — Tremont, Eden, and Mount Desert. The population is not far from seven thousand, and a large part of the island is under cultivation. The northern part especially is remarkable for rural beauty; but the center and southeast portions remain in native wildness, and are yet the haunt of the deer and the bear, though the latter animal is now rarely met with.

The sublime appearance of the island from the sea, on which its mountains are visible to a great distance, naturally attracted the attention of the earliest European navigators on our coast. According to some accounts, a French colony and mission was established there as early as 1608, on the western side of the Sound, and flourished for five years or more, till it was destroyed by the English. The first permanent settlement was made by Abraham Somes in 1761. The Sound, at the head of which he built his house, is to this day locally known as Somes's Sound.

Of late years, Mount Desert has become a favorite resort for artists and summer loungers. But it needs the hand of cultivated taste for the full development of its matchless natural beauties, which at present are to a great degree hidden by secondary growth. The "forest primeval" has been cut down, and the woods that have succeeded it have neither grandeur nor variety. Half a century of judicious clearing, and still more judicious sparing of the trees where they ought to be spared, would make this island, with its mighty cliffs and somber ravines and multitudinous ocean beaches, a place of pilgrimage from the ends of the earth.

SOMES'S SOUND

On the third day we rode back to the head of the Sound, where we found the Helen at anchor. We left the mare and the wagon in charge of the postmaster, and embarking, floated with the tide through scenery strikingly resembling the Hudson as it passes through the Highlands, to Southwest Harbor. Here the Assyrian and I went ashore to settle with the landlord for the use of his mare — not without some

217

misgivings, since we had not brought the animal back. The landlord, however, readily received our statement of the case, and said he could send for the animal when he wanted her. We all sat down upon a log near his premises, and, Yankee-like, whittled diligently while we discussed the terms of payment, which, after a lengthy session, were arranged liberally and satisfactorily.

We then made sail for Bar Harbor. The wind proving light and the currents adverse, we made little progress, and were twelve or fourteen hours in going as many miles. About sunset, as we slowly rounded Schooner Head, I picked up a baited cod-line and dropped it overboard, merely to occupy myself with pulling it in again. It had run out about two hundred feet, when, feeling a smart bite, I drew it up with a fine, lively haddock, weighing four pounds. This was the last of our sea-fishing. We reached the harbor at midnight, and our cruise was ended.

The next day I embarked on the steamer for Rockland and Boston, while the Artist and the Assyrian left the island by way of a bridge which connects Mount Desert with the mainland. The Professor and the seamen, after we bade them farewell, hoisted sail with a fair wind for Edgemoggin Reach, and thence back to Portland and Swampscott, where they arrived in due time.

It is related of the Caliph Abdalrahman, the mightiest and most magnificent of the Moorish monarchs of Spain, that he wrote toward the close of his life the following declaration: "I have now reigned above fifty years in victory or peace; beloved by my subjects, dreaded by my enemies, and respected by my allies. Riches and honors, power and pleasure, have waited on my call, nor does any earthly blessing appear to have been wanting to my felicity. In this situation, I have diligently numbered the days of pure and genuine happiness which have fallen to my lot; they amount to fourteen. O man! place not thy confidence in this present world!"

The Caliph Abdalrahman must have been hard to please. For my part, I can confidently say that during our cruise I enjoyed at least twice as many happy days as fell to the lot of his Majesty during his whole reign; and such, I am sure, would be the avowal of my friends the Professor, the Artist, and the Assyrian.

A NOTE ON THE ILLUSTRATIONS

The engravings in this book are the work of artists who saw the coast of New England at about the time Robert Carter did. They were carved into the end-grain of boxwood, which could withstand the printing of many thousands of copies. Chosen from a number of 19th Century books, they were reproduced here by means of offset lithography.

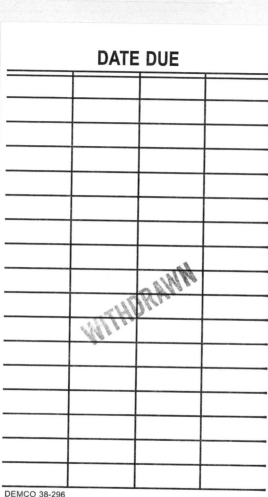

DATE DUE

WITHDRAWN

DEMCO 38-296